COME TOGETHER

TOGETHER

THE BUSINESS WISDOM OF

THE BEATLES

COME TOGETHER

TOGETHER

THE BUSINESS WISDOM OF

THE BEATLES

RICHARD COURTNEY   GEORGE CASSIDY

TURNER

Turner Publishing Company

445 Park Avenue, 9th Floor
New York, NY 10022
Phone: (646)291-8961   Fax: (646)291-8962

200 4th Avenue North, Suite 950
Nashville, TN 37219
Phone: (615)255-2665   Fax: (615)255-5081

www.turnerpublishing.com

Come Together: The Business Wisdom of the Beatles

Cover photo: courtesy Corbis Images

Library of Congress Cataloging-in-Publication Data

Courtney, Richard, 1954-
  Come together : the business wisdom of the Beatles / Richard Courtney and George
Cassidy.
    p. cm.
  ISBN 978-1-59652-808-6
1. Beatles--Finance. 2. Rock musicians--England--Biography. I. Cassidy, George, 1968-
II. Title.
  ML421.B4C69 2011
  782.42166092'2--dc22
  [B]
                                    2010042785

Printed in the United States of America

11 12 13 14 15 16 17 18 — 0 9 8 7 6 5 4 3 2 1

Richard dedicates this book to his brilliant and beautiful wife, Beth, who delivered his treasured Tom and Adeline about the time chapter 50 was completed. And to his mother-in-law, Veronica Strobel Seigenthaler, who tended the flock while chapters 50-100 were written. Special thanks to William Williams, Joey Molland, Shannon McCombs, and John, Paul, George, Ringo, and their supporting cast.

George dedicates this book to Hannah, George, and Henry.

Contents

Acknowledgments

George and Richard are eternally grateful to Joey Molland, Louise Harrison, Joe Johnson, Tony Bramwell, Richard Dodd, Chris Huston, Jack Oliver, Seth Swirsky, Ernie Winfrey, Barry Tashian, Ed Salamon, May Pang, Nancy Andrews, and Phil Kenzie for the interviews and to Geoff Emerick for visiting Nashville and presenting his story.

George and Richard thank each other. And Todd Bottorff for imagining.

Introduction

Why another book on the Beatles?

A fair enough question. After all, everyone knows the Beatles were a phenomenal success in their day—the crème de la crème of the music business. And their story has been told and retold at length many times. However, it is our belief that one crucial aspect of the Beatles' career has been largely ignored: their enormous value as models for running a business.

The premise of this book is quite simple: the steps that the Beatles took to become the most successful rock band of all time can be successfully applied to any business venture.

Their success was not a fluke, nor was it simply the inevitable result of their immense talent. *Come Together* chronicles the calculated and often brilliant effort that turned four teenaged greasers from Liverpool, England, into a multi-billion-dollar franchise with multigenerational appeal.

In 100 concise lessons, you will follow the steps taken by the Beatles to get to the top of their field time and time again for nearly fifty years. Along the way, you will see familiar episodes of Beatle history in a new light. And you will learn never-before-published insights gleaned through interviews with Beatle insiders like Joey Molland, Louise Harrison, Geoff Emerick, May Pang, Jack Oliver, Nancy Andrews, Chris Huston, and Tony Bramwell.

One caveat: this book isn't an uncritical valentine to the Fab Four. Beatle business wasn't always pretty. Where an honest critique is called for, we provide it. But this book dispels once and for all the myth that the Beatles, for all their musical brilliance, were bunglers in the business arena.

In the roughly fourteen years they were together, and long afterward, through cycles of failure and success, the Beatles encountered many of the same problems—and exhibited many of the managerial and operational behaviors—that more traditional businesses do. Your challenges were their challenges. Finally, in *Come Together,* the Beatles are unveiled as the ultimate business case study—one that will be of interest to any entrepreneur or Beatle fan.

1
You

If you wish to achieve Beatle-level success in your field, you must first learn to think like a Beatle. Because the Beatles were no accident. They wanted to be big. Bigger than Elvis. Bigger than anyone who went before, or came after. As you will learn, they took some hard knocks along the way. But they succeeded. The Fab Four became a global sensation. For all their missteps, and there were many, the Beatle business model has stood the test of time, as one of the most successful of all time.

If you truly think like a Beatle, take heart. You are in a very small minority. Few aspire to greatness, even fewer to be the greatest. Most around you are comfortable with mediocrity. Others may achieve success, even set records and receive awards with their performances. Many simply want to be big enough to receive a regular paycheck. You, however, will not be satisfied until you have taken a shot at the top.

John Lennon was born with the drive and desire to be the best in the world—at something—and became aware of this blessing, or affliction, in his early teens. But his dreams remained vague—and therefore unattainable—until he and his young friend Paul McCartney began hearing American rock and roll records. The songs of Buddy Holly, Elvis, Ray Charles, the Everly Brothers, and Little Richard transformed their inchoate longings for something different, something better, something bigger, into a passion and gradually a plan.

We all know when we meet or see someone who has that spark, from Steve Jobs at Apple Computers to cycling icon Lance Armstrong. They seem to be having the time of their lives, and they are *kicking butt.* That was the Beatles. They couldn't have brought the same verve, the same brilliance, to anything but their music.

In life and in business, finding your passion, your mission, your bliss—is the single biggest distinguishing factor between Beatles-style success and a world of also-rans. Think of it this way. There is a powerful engine inside you that is designed to do only one thing. Once you harness its power, it is self-sustaining, motivational, miraculous. It makes success almost inevitable. One need only find the ignition switch. Some of us, the lucky few, are born knowing where the switch is. The rest of us must do some work to find it.

So, how do you find the switch? By understanding you. First, there are your genes. You are he—your father—as you are she, your mother. And you are they, blessed with the talents and virtues and struggling with all the weaknesses and limitations that they have imparted to you.

The Beatles were no different. John Lennon was taught to play the guitar by his mother, Julia, who played the banjo and taught him his first chords banjo-style. In addition to her musical abilities, the gregarious Julia possessed a keen, quick wit and was more of a friend to her son than a mother. This relationship shaped the personality of John Lennon and started him on his way. Tragically, she was hit and killed by a car driven by an off-duty police officer while standing at a bus stop when John was only seventeen. Yet, even this great loss seemed to fuel his ambition and his muse.

Paul McCartney likewise had a musical pedigree. He was the son of Jim McCartney, a cotton salesman who was also an accomplished musician and led the Jimmy Mac Jazz Band in his spare time. The elder McCartney became proficient on a number of instruments, as did his son Paul, an aptitude no doubt inherited from his father.

After family, there is your community, the environment. The other people and places that went before. Some are dead and some are living. The "we" who are all together—this is also part of you.

For the Beatles, it was Liverpool, a bustling port city that overflowed with creativity, satire, and music—there were more than 300 bands in Liverpool in the late 1950s and early 1960s. The American rock and roll records sailors stowed away as ballast and brought home to Liverpool became the fodder for the Beatles' teenage dreams. It has also been said that infants born to Liverpudlians are not taught to walk or to "toddle," but to swagger. It was that insouciant attitude with which "the lads" charmed the world.

Chances are, when you consider the sum of your background and experiences, you have an idea—or at least a nagging feeling—about what it is you were made to do. That feeling is your business, your calling, your *life*—waiting to be born.

I hope you find it nice meeting you.

2

The Concept

You have the gift. Is it a curse or a blessing? Esteemed author Philip Norman wrote the definitive Beatles biography *Shout*, as well as the most highly regarded work on John Lennon. Norman quoted Lennon as saying, "I'm a genius or I'm mad. Which is it?" So now you know yourself what you're meant to do, be it genius or madness. What next?

Begin. And be strong. To enjoy the success you seek, you must have the courage and fortitude to beat a different path from that of anyone you know. You will need to call on all of your knowledge, all of your experiences, and open yourself to outside influences. If you need a partner, find one. Use extreme scrutiny and be prepared to have a few trials and numerous errors in the process. Don't settle for second fiddle.

At fifteen, John Lennon already had his concept—his "tree" if you will—the one that would define his life. As he fell under the spell of rock and roll music, he knew deep in his soul that he wanted to form the greatest rock and roll band in the history of the world. Somewhere deep down, he knew he *would* form such a band. Lennon thought he had it in his first band the Quarrymen, whose motto was "Quarry Men! Strong Before Our Birth." Perhaps Lennon possessed that quality, but the others were not even in his forest, certainly not his tree.

Simultaneously, unbeknown to John, only a few miles away, a person of equal ambition and the skills to go along with it was honing his talents and setting his sights. This person, Paul McCartney, would become half of arguably the greatest songwriting team of all time. Is there a partner in your tree? Check the branches.

As he drifted further and further into this dream, John's Aunt Mimi, his legal guardian, worried for her truant nephew. She nagged him to apply himself to his studies—or, failing that, to get a proper job. But even then, Lennon knew that he was special, that he had a talent—a gift—not shared by others. Perhaps even more important, he had the dogged self-belief to begin, and to stick with it through thick and thin. The thing is, Mimi was, in some sense, correct. She wet her finger, stuck it in the wind, and made a sensible call about which way the wind was blowing. She was not, however, standing in Lennon's tree. Lennon picked his tree—one in which few others could see any prospect of success—and then implemented his strategy tirelessly.

Does this sound familiar? It should. It's common to great success stories in all walks of business. Like Bill Gates dropping out of Harvard to start Microsoft, or Hewlett and Packard tinkering in the garage while their dinners grew cold.

If you are going to conquer your industry, you must find an uninhabited tree. The competition can be perched on a tree nearby, but not yours. How many books have been written on the Beatles? More than likely, more than a thousand, but there is none like this one. As a real estate columnist and a songwriter, we found a tree and climbed it. You will be amazed at the fruit our tree is bearing, one of which is this book. John Lennon and Paul McCartney, from their respective perches in their own particular tree, were getting ready to change the world.

To reach your potential, look for that one special concept. Find your tree.

3
A Little Help from Your Friends

By now you are itching to get started, aren't you? Well, slow down. And please don't be offended when we tell you this—you need serious help. Whether you are just starting your business, or are bogged down in running your existing business, the biggest mistake you can make is trying to do it all yourself.

John Lennon needed help, and he knew it. On July 6, 1957, sixteen-year-old John, after a set by his first combo, the Quarrymen, met a younger lad of fifteen who amazed them all with a polished version of "Twenty Flight Rock" by Eddie Cochran. Lennon immediately realized that this lucky meeting held the key to success. He had found his partner, someone who could hold down the chords so Lennon could be—well, Lennon.

Lennon asked McCartney to join the Quarrymen. McCartney, impressed with Lennon's showmanship and authentic rock and roll attitude, accepted. Paul realized that John offered an effusiveness that he lacked. Paul understood that his quest for perfection could at times prove to be a hindrance. That same day backstage, Paul impressed John with his ability to tune a guitar, a skill John had failed to hone up to that time.

On Paul's first encounter with John at the Woolton Fete, he watched John perform songs for which he had not taken time to learn the lyrics, rather making them up as he went along. Not only did Lennon improvise, his improvisations were hilariously twisted. In his version of the Del Vikings' "Come Go with Me," John added the line "Come little darling, come go with me to the penitentiary."

Then came a little Beatle bootstrapping. In order to staff the group, they did as all startups do: they went to those they knew well. John enlisted his best friend from art school, Stuart (Stu) Sutcliffe, to play the bass. Paul snagged his own young pal, George Harrison, who was even better than Paul at the guitar.

Having someone who could focus on the things that were challenging for one member of the band, while another focused on the things he did well, was one of the foundational elements of the Beatles' success. John Lennon would not have achieved worldwide prominence as a musician without McCartney as his personal and musical foil. In retrospect, it seems that McCartney kept Lennon from becoming too acerbic, while Lennon's edge complemented Paul's penchant for pop. Lennon and McCartney served each other in a student-mentor role, each learning from, and teaching, the other.

With McCartney at his back, Lennon could do the things he did best and let McCartney fill in the gaps. And without some timely help from their friends, they would have remained no more than two talented dreamers. Instead, they became a band, eventually adding Ringo Starr, whose steady hand at the drums provided the foundational beat for the songs. With George Harrison's vocal harmonies and guitar fills complementing each composition, the Beatles had become more than the sum of their parts.

The world is not going to beat a path to your door. To get off the ground, you will need to do as the early Beatles did: seek among your business and personal acquaintances those who have the skills you lack, and for the necessary manpower and logistical reach that you need.

It worked for Warren Buffett and Charlie Munger at Berkshire Hathaway, and Rogers and Hammerstein, and Apple's Steve Jobs and Steve Wozniak. It will work for you. Find someone who can tune your ideas.

4

Leadership

Think of any enormously successful company. Can you picture the leader of that company? Chances are, you *can*. Amazon and Jeff Bezos. Wendy's and Dave Thomas. Chrysler and Lee Iacocca. Wal-Mart and Sam Walton. To quote Leadership Nashville founder Nelson Andrews, "The parks are filled with statues erected in honor of leaders, but have you ever seen a statue commemorating a committee?" There is always a strong leader. Someone who took command, who controlled and guided the company on its path to success. Failing that, someone who set an example and demonstrated how to be a success.

By contrast look at a company that is set up as a "democracy" and you see an enterprise that is dying a slow and painful death.

Decisions are made slowly and by committee. Strategy is hashed and rehashed endlessly, and very little actual work gets done. Most of us have been there at one time or another. Perhaps you are shuddering right now at the memory.

It was no different for the Beatles. In the beginning, John Lennon was clearly the leader of the Beatles. Though he was not necessarily the most talented vocally or instrumentally, he was their general and their cheerleader. Through his fierce intelligence and force of personality, he established the character and direction of the group and drove it. Equally important, all members of the band, including the talented and headstrong Paul, allowed themselves to be led. They all followed his vision. If they had been second-guessing his every decision at the outset, behaving like a committee, there would have been no Beatles.

If you are the leader of your enterprise, lead. If you are not the leader, follow. You have nothing to lose but a little time by staking out your position: the only alternative is certain failure and the ebb tide of obscurity.

5

Working Like a Dog

Are you the Beatles? Or are you a one-hit wonder? Talented, but essentially a dreamer and day-tripper, ready to take the easy way out? There is only one way to find out. And that's by working like a dog. There is no substitute for hard work. Think of the athlete: he may wake up sore, but after a few hours he is itching to practice again. To get it right.

As a boy, John Lennon began his musical career playing a cheap guitar tuned like a banjo. Paul McCartney first learned music on a trumpet before switching to guitar. George Harrison worked his way through guitar manuals. Ringo Starr, though not yet in the picture, was teaching himself to play on a drum kit his mother purchased for him. All four continued to learn the basic mechanics of music and playing their instruments throughout the late 1950s. But as their teenage years began to wane, they were not on track to become world-beaters in their early twenties. Not just yet. To become the Beatles, they needed a pressure cooker. A real "do or die" situation. They needed Hamburg.

In 1960, the group, which had taken to calling itself the Beatles (a punning homage to Buddy Holly's Crickets and to beat music) were booked to play in Hamburg, Germany. Once there, they performed eight hours a day, seven days a week—sets at 3:00 p.m., 11:00 p.m., 2:00 a.m., and 4:00 a.m. Playing in a sleazy club located in the red-light district of a town filled with prostitutes, strippers, and drunken sailors, the Beatles learned to Beatle. To placate the sometimes violent denizens of this twilight world, the Beatles learned to *Mach Shau,* German for "make show." They learned and performed reams of material under duress, on-the-job. They were in a constant state of physical exhaustion, beaten to a psychological pulp. And—gradually—they became *good.*

The Beatles were not the first or the only Liverpool band to make the trek. Canny German club owners also booked Gerry and the Pacemakers, the Undertakers, and Rory Storm and the Hurricanes, among others, from Liverpool's seemingly bottomless well of hard-working talent. In this light, perhaps too much has been made recently about how the sheer number of performances in Hamburg provided the Beatles with some sort of statistical edge that fueled their later successes. Almost certainly, no other Liverpool band in Hamburg was as erratic and unformed as the embryonic Beatles were when they began their stint. They underwent a remarkable transformation, returning from a total of two trips to Hamburg with a distinctive style that would soon earn them a spot as one of the top two or three bands in Liverpool.

For most startup businesses, there is initially weak—or nonexistent—demand for the products or services of that business. The Beatles were no different. Through long hours of sweat and toil, flying at the edge of their abilities and beyond, the Beatles simultaneously created both their distinctive product *and* a market for it.

The world doesn't know it needs you—yet. Seek out the proving ground, the crucible, the ordeal. It will raise your game, accelerate your progress, and prepare you to go all the way. Work a hard day's night. Work like a dog. Eight days a week, if possible. It's the only way to find out if you have the appetite for success. And you'll find out if the world has an appetite for you.

6

"Direct from Hamburg"

When the Beatles returned to Liverpool from Hamburg, something had changed. Work had been scarce before they left, but they found they were suddenly in demand.

The secret? One of the most simple and ingenious marketing subterfuges of the twentieth century. Because the Beatles were billed as "Direct from Hamburg," people thought they were a German group. Suddenly, they stuck out from among the 300 or so other bands crowding Liverpool's bustling music scene. Curious rock and roll fans suddenly thronged their shows, hungry for the best in Continental beat music.

And when the new version of the Beatles hit the stage, they didn't disappoint. It was a polished group that had the ability to

Mach Shau—and then some. The local audiences were not prepared for what they heard or saw, but they knew that they loved it. The Beatles had arrived in England.

It's worth mentioning that just before this swift uptick in their fortunes, the Beatles had been ready to pack it in. Their adventure in Hamburg had ended unceremoniously in a flurry of contact disputes, deportations, romantic entanglements, and insolvency. Back in Liverpool, exhausted and not a little discouraged, they rested and regrouped. But when they did reemerge, they found that their hard work in Hamburg had, improbably enough, created a local market in Liverpool ripe for their music. "Direct from Hamburg" turned out to be a sort of shorthand for all the hard-won confidence and skill they now brought to their music.

Like the Beatles, you have your product or service, and it's good. How do you build credibility and convince people they want it? What is a convincing, intriguing shorthand for your edge, the thing that sets you apart from the crowd in your industry?

Find your "Direct from Hamburg."

7

Image and Branding

Are you ready for your close-up? A distinctive visual identity in the marketplace can be as important as—or more important than—anything else. You can succeed without it—but not on a world-changing, era-defining level. Think about it. Coca-Cola. The Volkswagen Beetle. The iPhone. And yes, the Beatles.

The Beatles' visual identity would evolve over their career, but there was one element of their persona which inspired an unprecedented amount of conversation, press coverage, and imitation right out of the gate. No, not the music. The *haircuts.* You remember them, don't you? "Mop tops"—longish hair, combed over the ears and forward over the temple and forehead. In a world of crew cuts, "duck tails," and "short back and sides," the longer hair made quite a splash.

As they did in many other instances, the Beatles hit upon this crucial element of their success by simply being alert to what was going on around them. In Hamburg, the Beatles had struck up an acquaintance with two young Germans, Astrid Kirchherr and her boyfriend Klaus Voormann. At the time, Astrid had created a stylish haircut for Klaus that covered his one slight physical shortcoming: his large ears.

First Stuart Sutcliffe, then George Harrison, adopted the new style. John, Paul, and then-drummer Pete Best would have no part of it, and continued to wear their hair combed back and full of grease in the style of their hero, Elvis. It was some time before John and Paul succumbed to what would become known worldwide as the "Beatle haircut." (Pete Best never did—but that's a story for another chapter.)

The Beatles had the musical goods, to be sure. But by the time they were ready for their close-up, they were a distinctive and visually arresting presence as well. This contributed as much as anything else to their rapid ascent.

Does your business have a distinctive visual identity? If not, it's time to find something—a logo, a color scheme, even a *haircut*—that people can identify instantly with your product or service.

8

Thinning the Ranks

Have you ever had to fire a friend? Do you think you could? If you've followed this book so far, chances are you have several friends and acquaintances working with you or providing crucial support in some way. At this point, you may look around you and notice that some of these people—whose help was so vital at the beginning—have begun to lose interest, to lag behind, to slow you down. If so, it's high time to thank them for their help up to this point, and show them the door. This is not the time for anything to be slowing you down—not even friendship.

During their second trip to Hamburg, the Beatles began to recognize that they were becoming minor stars. They had built a following and been invited to participate as the backing band on a

German recording session for Tony Sheridan, another British performer. The session spawned a minor German hit record called "My Bonnie." With a certain sense of satisfaction, the boys surely realized that they had all come quite a long way. All of them, that is, except Stuart Sutcliffe.

Stu was a highly regarded artist who had more interest in painting than in music. While the other Beatles were obsessively honing their musical skills, Stu had fallen in love with Astrid Kirchherr (who had invented the Beatles' haircut). As a result, he still possessed only rudimentary skills on the bass—fumbling around at low volumes and often turning his back to the audience to hide that he might be playing in a different key than the others.

This was not good enough for Paul, who determined—correctly—that for the band to reach the next level, it must jettison Stu and have a proper bass player—namely, himself. Out of loyalty, John at first insisted that Stu remain in the group. In the end, however, all three men agreed that the Beatles were better without Stu and he left the band. In fact, Stu was grateful that he was now free to pursue his painting and enjoy more time with Astrid.

Be prepared to be ruthless in your assessment of what needs to happen to move your business forward, *and* in the actions you take based on that assessment. Listen to stakeholders—like Paul McCartney—who feel moved to step forward with honest and heartfelt criticism. The future of your business is at stake. If the Beatles had not dropped Stu, they would never have moved beyond the clubs. And if Paul hadn't had the gumption to challenge Lennon—ditto.

There is risk. Friendships may or may not survive no matter what course you take. Keep in mind that true friends—like Stu—will understand when their interests and yours no longer coincide, and move on gracefully.

9

Setting Up Shop

Do your customers know where to find you? The Beatles made a second trip to Hamburg in 1961. Upon their return, the Beatles began to establish themselves as one of the best bands in Liverpool, if not *the* best band. They took up professional residency in a club called the Cavern, so-called because it was a cavern. This subterranean vault, with its extremely hot temperatures and cramped, dank space, had been used up to that point mainly for jazz performances. To add insult to injury, the management hired the Beatles to play the lunchtime shift—hardly peak hours.

As in Hamburg, the Beatles could have balked at the drab surroundings for their dream. But they didn't. And as it turned out, the Cavern had several things to recommend it, the most important being its location in the city center (in America, "downtown"). This represented a definitive leap upward in the strict hierarchy of the Liverpool music scene, which began in the surrounding community centers, pubs, and church halls, before proceeding to ballrooms and clubs in the city center. The Beatles were now one of only two dozen or so bands (out of 300, remember) playing regularly downtown.

The Cavern became ground zero for the Beatles' stratospheric rise. The venue was soon packed each day. In only a few months, it would be impossible for the Cavern to accommodate the crowds the Beatles would draw. And the fact that the Beatles were able to draw so well at this uncomfortable venue convinced other dance halls and clubs in the area to hire this hard-rocking band with the funny haircuts. Not least in importance, the Cavern was close to NEMS, the department store owned by the family of a young man named Brian Epstein who would play the pivotal role in the next phase of the Beatles' career. (More on this in the next chapter!)

Location, location, location. It's not a unique story. Rumor has it that Tom Carvel, the ice cream franchise king, bought his first ice cream store after his ice cream *truck* broke down and he found that he sold more ice cream sitting in one place. From such humble beginnings—dank basements and broken down trucks—markets are created and empires are born.

Don't hide from success. The establishment of a home base, be it ever so humble, is vitally important. Make sure once they know your name, they can look up the number. Make sure your customers can find you.

10

Fire Yourself and Hire a Manager

We have contemplated the possibility of firing your friends. But are you ready to fire *yourself*? At some point, you're going to have to. You've got a full plate and there are still new markets and new territories to conquer. Chances are you may have reached a point where you simply lack the contacts or know-how to take things to the next level. The answer is simple: Fire yourself. Hire a manager.

By late 1962, the Beatles were hitting on all cylinders. In the midst of their conquest of Liverpool, they were approached by Brian Epstein. He was the manager of the North End Music Store, a record shop set within a larger store owned by his family. A failed actor, his greatest pleasure and success to date had come in creating the store's window arrangements, for which he had an undeniable flair.

The story that was widely circulated was that someone had come into NEMS and asked for a copy of "My Bonnie" by the Beatles (the record they had made in Hamburg with Tony Sheridan). Epstein, in his zeal to stock the proper inventory, investigated the Beatles by attending one of their Cavern performances (the Cavern was close by). After the show, floored by their raw talent, he approached them and asked them to allow him to manage them. If the record shop story is true, perhaps the most striking thing is that Epstein went in there to find out how to stock a minor German hit record and came out managing what would become the biggest band in the world. That surely ranks as one of the key entrepreneurial coups of the modern age. But it also speaks to how the flimsiest causal chain of events can change history.

Without Epstein's inexperienced but enthusiastic management, the Beatles would never have gotten out of the clubs. They gave him obedience (see chapter 2 for more on the benefits of following the leader), and in return he dedicated himself to their success. He cleaned up their rough edges and made them ready for prime time. And whether out of incompetence or brilliance, or some combination of the two, Epstein did not book his new clients into steady and lucrative rounds of regional or national ballroom work. (This is what happened to many of the other top bands in Liverpool, such as the Undertakers.) Instead, the Beatles continued to work at the Cavern, lived hand-to-mouth, and used their time off to pursue a recording deal. History has rendered its verdict on the wisdom of this decision!

It's important that the new blood is in your corner. The relationship should be one of mutual benefit—but make sure you are hiring someone who is going to look out for your interests—who is going to do every little thing *for you.*

It is important to note that in order for this to happen, John—whose leadership had brought them to this point—essentially had to resign and become "one of the lads." Though still first among equals, he surely knew that he himself did not have the mojo to get the boys a record deal down in London. Epstein just might. Though he might not have been able to articulate the distinction, a clear distinction was emerging between John's *leadership* of the Beatles, and the *management* skills necessary to propel their career forward.

Many a hapless entrepreneur—unable to make such a distinction—finds himself effectively "fired" just when things are taking off. A common example is when the infusion of angel or venture capital brings with it a new set of managers. If the entrepreneur is unable to cede the necessary ground, or to understand properly her new role in the newly expanded organization, it's a short slide off the cc: email list. Fire yourself and hire a replacement who shares your vision, but who takes charge of scaling up your organization.

So when you have hit the wall and don't know how to get past it, maybe it's time to fire yourself and hire a manager. If you are lucky, you will get someone like the supremely entrepreneurial Brian Epstein—someone who can take care of the details, provide sound strategic advice, *and* pick out your snazzy new wardrobe.

11
Capitalization

Do you know the reason most companies fail? A little thing called lack of capital. Money can't buy you love, but it sure can keep your business afloat. In the incubation stage of any business, it must exist on a bare-bones budget until the profits begin to roll in. Cash flow is the immediate concern. However, as things progress, there must be working capital placed in reserve. Some of the cash that flows in must be set aside for capital expenditures and other large or irregular expenses, not to mention improvements and upgrades to your business.

Before Brian Epstein arrived, the four Beatles—John, Paul, George, and Pete—had cash coming in from their regular engagements. However, it is fair to say that none of the Beatles was setting aside much for a rainy day. Moreover, each man handled his own expenses. For example, each was responsible for buying his own instrument and for any equipment or services required to maintain it. In the process of doing so, all four had incurred debts at Hessey's, the local Liverpool music store.

This is another reason why the appearance of Brian Epstein was so fortuitous. Epstein arranged to pay off these debts. He understood that the strain of financial obligations could eventually cause the Beatles to lose focus on their music. He also set up an accounting plan wherein their earnings were pooled, their expenses paid, and the Beatles themselves were paid a weekly salary. He also bought them new clothes for their appearances out of the reserves in this Beatle fund.

It is fortunate for the Beatles that they had less overhead than many businesses. They generally lived with their families, or as quasi-homeless squatters in the Bambi Kino in Hamburg. Their transportation as they crisscrossed the hinterlands of England was a van that had no windshield. In the dead of winter, it was so cold that whoever wasn't driving was stacked one on top of the other, so that at least the person on the bottom of the pile was warm. They rotated the Beatle sandwich regularly when it reached the point that the top Beatle was nearly frozen.

Take a page out of their book. Although frostbite is generally a bad idea, avoid relying too heavily on debt to finance your daily operations or growth. History has shown again and again that businesses built on debt can survive when times are good, but they are the first to go when times are bad and the debt can no longer be serviced.

Don't count on being lucky. Be smart instead. To build lasting success with a measure of independence from business cycles, create your own capital reserves as early as you can.

12
Failure

You have proved you're a dreamer, and you're willing to work hard and sacrifice for your dream. To suffer, even. But are you ready for failure? Bleak, soul-crushing, humiliating, and perhaps *public* failure? I certainly hope so. Because if you're a perfectionist, you will be afraid to fail. You will avoid it. And if you do experience failure, it will so dishearten you that you will give up just as you are *really* getting down to business. And you will never taste the elixir of Beatle-style success.

So far we have followed the path of the Beatles from their inception through their domination of Liverpool. Great success awaited . . . but the Beatles had not tasted failure for the last time. Brian Epstein, secure in his role as manager, dedicated his life to the pursuit of a recording contract for "the boys," as he fondly called them. His efforts were rewarded when Dick Rowe at Decca records agreed to an audition for the Beatles. The Beatles were excited. This was it! They had made it. They knew they were good . . . no, great. Once Decca heard their sound, they'd flip. But as it turned out, Rowe rejected them, believing (as he famously told Epstein) that guitar groups were somewhat old hat.

It's hard to overstate the impact this had on the Beatles. With the grail in hand, at the last second it was dashed from their lips. This was not like getting kicked out of Hamburg—the whole world was lousy with seedy dives where the Beatles could play, and besides, that was not their ultimate goal. There were only a handful of major record companies in England. For the first time, their options were narrowing, not widening. The Beatles felt that their years of work, playing in the worst and the best of venues, all of the cleaning up, the new clothes, and everything else—all had been flushed down the toilet. They were devastated. Brian felt as if he had failed them.

At this point, feeling foolish in their matching suits, lesser men might have told Dick Rowe to stuff it and then packed it in. Not the Beatles. Brian went straight to working the phones. The lads went back to the Cavern to work even harder. John and Paul decided they would write better songs. Six months later, they would have their record contract.

Do not fear failure. It is an integral part of any enterprise. Research the history of any company that has achieved lasting success and you will find at least one major failure along the way. Or many.

The Model T was not Henry Ford's first automobile—just the first to succeed on a massive scale. And the Ford Motor Company later lost a mint on the Edsel.

It is not a question of if, the question is when. Failure will come. The companies that have succeeded on a grand scale respond well to failure and bounce back stronger than before. Think of "New" Coke. Before its introduction, Coke had been losing market share. After its introduction, and the retirement of the original formula, the Coca-Cola company faced rising consumer anger in addition to sales that were still, well, kind of flat. It was only after Coke retrenched and reintroduced the original formula that a grateful public returned the brand firmly to the leadership position it still enjoys today.

Although they had no way of knowing this at the time, the Beatles were about to bounce back—and bounce high. And what, you may ask, of Dick Rowe? How does one recover from the very public humiliation of letting the Beatles slip through one's fingers? Very nicely, it turns out. About a year after this horrendous gaffe, working on a tip from George Harrison, he signed another guitar combo from London. Their name, you ask? The Rolling Stones.

13

The Accidental Mentor

Are you keeping faith with your destiny? The odds are that you are experiencing the success (or lack thereof) that you deserve. In other words, if you're waiting for your lucky break, don't hold your breath. In Beatle terms, *there is no such thing as a lucky break.* Many aspects of the Beatles' success seem lucky or accidental on first inspection. Some are, but most aren't. Upon closer inspection, many of these lucky "breaks" reveal themselves as the almost inevitable by-products of hard work and perseverance.

Take George Martin. Brian Epstein eventually succeeded in scheduling another audition for the Beatles, this time with Martin, who had recently been given the authority to sign acts at Parlophone, an EMI subsidiary. During the audition, Martin attempted to find the "front man" of the group, in the mold of Bill Haley and the Comets, Buddy Holly and the Crickets, or Rory Storm and the Hurricanes. He soon realized that the Beatles didn't fit that mold. But he liked what he saw. Aside from their promising musicianship and songwriting talent, he was impressed by their sense of humor and their charm. Like Epstein before him, he was moved to take a risk on these hard-charging, undeniably talented boys.

On its face, the pairing made little sense. Parlophone specialized in comedy records. Martin, thirty-six, was a classically trained record producer. He had worked with the cast of the *Goon Show,* a popular radio comedy, including rising star Peter Sellers (a hero of Lennon's), but he had absolutely no rock and roll or pop experience.

At first, Martin as producer merely polished the Beatles for the marketplace. The market is not interested in talent or potential. It wants what it can judge with its eyes, ears, nose, and mouth. What it can hold in its hands. Martin knew this and the Beatles were putty in *his* hands. Soon enough, Martin's classical training and experience working with unconventional comedic talents like Peter Sellers would make their mark on Beatle records. They were among the first rock and roll bands to feature orchestral and chamber ensemble arrangements in their music. They also employed a wide range of zany sound effects in their music, many of them from the studio's expansive comedy sound effects library. George Martin and the Beatles created a kind of positive feedback loop. He made them sound better, which challenged them to be better. The result was the most outstanding (and perhaps the most lucrative) catalog of recorded music in history.

This unlikely, magical pairing of George Martin and the Beatles seems lucky in retrospect, if not downright accidental. But it most certainly was not. Brian Epstein's unflagging efforts made it *inevitable* that the Beatles and George Martin would have their mutual audition.

There are no accidents, only hard work and preparation meeting opportunity. You probably know that Ray Kroc took McDonald's from a single California restaurant to a worldwide fast-food powerhouse. But did you know that Kroc had no interest in selling hamburgers? The franchise began as a scheme for Kroc, a milkshake mixer salesman, to create a ready market for the machines. Certainly, his plan succeeded beyond his wildest dreams, but there was nothing lucky or accidental about it. Kroc had most likely been in and out of hundreds or even thousands of burger joints, diners, and drugstores before he hit upon his idea.

Whether you're a rock band looking to make a record with a classically trained producer of comedy records, or a milkshake mixer salesman opening a burger joint, there is no avenue too unlikely for success. And when you're looking to turn your talent and potential into something the market can digest—literally or figuratively—you do well to keep in mind this Beatle mantra: *there are no lucky breaks.*

14
Being Bested

If I were writing a thriller about the Beatles, the plot twist at this juncture would be that there is a double agent in their midst. He is the only man who can stop them from becoming a world phenomenon. He must be found—and stopped—before it is too late. His name? Pete Best.

Poor Pete Best, you say? The handsome drummer jettisoned in favor of Ringo just before the group hit the stratosphere? Why pick on him? After their EMI audition, George Martin told Brian Epstein that Pete's timekeeping was not steady enough to play on commercial records. A short time later, Epstein unceremoniously informed Best that he was out.

It would be fair to say that Best didn't see it coming. He had a substantial female following in Liverpool, where he was billed as "mean, moody, and magnificent." His mother Mona had provided the Beatles with crucial early gigs at the Casbah, the youth club she ran out of the basement of the Best home. The single Mona was even dating one of the Beatles' closest friends and unofficial "road manager," Neil Aspinall, at the time.

Best got the gig just before their departure to Hamburg, based on his personal acquaintance with the Beatles through the Casbah club. But during their time in Hamburg, the Beatles would occasionally jam with members of other bands, including the very polished drummer for Rory Storm and the Hurricanes. This fellow, who had an impressive beard and sideburns and gaudy rings on several of his fingers, called himself Ringo Starr. They got on like gangbusters. And the Beatles (at least three of them) thought he was the coolest man they'd ever seen or heard. A real professional musician, with a cool stage name to boot.

When they returned from their second visit to Hamburg, John, Paul, and George *looked* different, having adopted the Klaus Voormann haircut. Pete Best, however, looked the same. He drummed the same. He was the same. As John, Paul, and George began (literally and figuratively) to march to the beat of a different drummer, Pete Best chose the road he had always traveled.

He had always been different from the others—as the billing went, mean, moody, and magnificent—where the others were curious, funny, sarcastic, and quick-witted. This difference in style and temperament only grew with time. If Best was unaware of it, the other Beatles weren't. Martin's comment was probably a last straw. With a recording contract in hand, they could now cherry-pick Ringo away from his plush gig with Rory Storm, something they may have had in mind for a while. He would have to adopt the Beatle haircut and lose the beard, but he could keep his sideburns.

It's easy to feel sorry for Pete Best. Of all the Beatles and Beatle associates we've met so far, he suffered one of the cruelest fates. Imagine decades of flinching as every Beatles' song comes on the radio, feeling the humiliation and the sting of rejection and the bile rising in the pit of your stomach. Nothing he could ever do or be would equal what he might have done or been as a Beatle. It is no wonder that Best attempted suicide.

The business of greatness is equal parts triumph and tragedy. It is difficult to sugarcoat Pete Best's personal tragedy—a man overcome unawares by his own nature at the cusp of greatness—with a business moral. And yet, there are two things worth considering. One is that you should always have an exit strategy. If you are reading this book, it is unlikely that you will play the Pete Best role in the saga of your business, but it is still an unhappy fact of life that many business relationships end badly. No matter how much you love what you do, you should know what's next—for your own sanity.

The second thing to consider is this: had George Martin allowed Pete to stay, there would be no Ringo. No Ringo, no Beatles. Not as we know them, anyway. Not four lovable moptops, but three lovable moptops and one mean, moody, magnificent greaser. No "Yellow Submarine." No "With a Little Help from My Friends." For Pete Best to stay, all of the relentless, self-improving urges the

Beatles had pursued would somehow have to be quieted—an impossibility. To say that he alone could have stopped the Beatles from being the worldwide historic success they became is not to stretch the truth. Pete Best *had* to go. It was only a matter of time.

Perhaps that fact could finally set Pete Best free.

15
Customer Service

Do you love your customers? The Beatles did. They loved their fans, and they realized the fans were their customers. They took the time to answer every fan letter possible and signed thousands upon thousands of autographs. They were accessible—at least in the early days—playing date after date after date, sometimes singing every song they knew.

They went to great extremes to provide their public with the best service possible. They responded from the stage to the whims of the screaming fans with gestures and winks; even John Lennon's sometimes bizarre antics, like the quasi-spastic stamping and clapping which he first began to effect in Hamburg, endeared them to the hearts of their fans. They ate up the japery, knowing that in his own, inimitable way, Lennon was reaching out to them.

It's fair to say that the Beatles moved heaven and earth for their fans, at least once. At their first performance in the United States, in Washington, D.C., they played on a rotating stage surrounded on all sides by screaming fans. After several numbers, they realized that the rotating stage was not rotating—and the fans behind them had only seen their backs. The Beatles interrupted their set, and then turned the rotating stage themselves, using only Beatle elbow grease and almost wrenching their backs in the process. *That's* service.

Customer retention is one of the most important aspects of business. Gaining a customer is difficult and expensive. Retaining one customer costs less and can be the equivalent, profit-wise, of earning many new customers. The Beatles were masters of customer retention. All three volumes of their *Anthology* debuted at number one in the charts in the mid-1990s, a quarter century after they broke up. And their compilation of number-one hits, titled simply *1*, also debuted at number one over thirty years after they broke up. *That's* customer loyalty. Grown men and women break into tears when Paul McCartney dips into the Beatles catalog at one of his concerts. *That's* customer loyalty.

They earned it in those early days of scraping and hustling to make contact with their fans. The Beatles had a product, to be sure—their music, which was unique and wonderful and pulled people in. But their customer service was what kept people loyal to the Beatles. If they had been rude, inaccessible jerks, people would have written them off, no matter how wonderful their music.

You may never have screaming teenage girls lined up around the block for a glimpse of your product or service. But once you have customers, don't neglect them in favor of new sales. That's the fool's road. No matter what your business, the love you take will always equal the love you make.

16

Communication

What is the one thing that your business could not survive without? If you are thinking of your product or service, or your cash flow, or infrastructure such as telephones and computers, *wrong*. Take a step back. The answer, no matter who you are and what you do, is *people*. Even if you are a one-man operation, you still must persuade other people to buy what you're selling. There is no level of automation or technological innovation that can remove this emotional X factor from the heart of your business. That makes an effective communication strategy—internal and external—just about job number one, doesn't it?

Think about it. Why is eBay the quintessential Internet business, while all manner of online grocery and pet stores have gone the way of the telegraph? Because eBay is fundamentally about *people.* People all around the world connecting to buy and sell. If you're wondering if anybody in the world wants your collection of Ringo Starr bobbleheads, eBay lets you connect with the people who do—whether it's a young Beatles fan in the Czech Republic, or Ringo himself. At the heart of eBay is communication—asking questions, negotiating, giving and receiving feedback keeps everybody honest.

Communication should be at the heart of your business as well. Effective communication is one of the best safeguards of productivity and profitability. And poor communication will eventually, inevitably, cost you a lot of money. Neglected customers and employees move on and you are forced to deal with the higher costs of hiring new employees and making new sales. You will spend your time repairing, rather than growing, your business.

Immediately after signing the Beatles, Brian Epstein put systems into place that forced weekly communication between him and his new clients. In these weekly briefings or memos, he identified upcoming dates for which he had booked the group, communications he had made on their behalf, as well as any miscellaneous items that he felt should be addressed.

Epstein continued in this manner up until the Beatles ceased touring in 1966. This system had two benefits. The obvious one was that the Beatles knew what was going on at any particular time— there were no missed gigs or other unpleasant surprises. The second, and perhaps more significant, benefit was that the system motivated Epstein to maintain forward momentum. If there were no new business on any given week, it would have been instantly obvious that Epstein was slacking off or coasting. He was required to have done something to promote the band each week, lest he incur the wrath of the Beatles in general, and Lennon, whom he adored, in particular.

This level of organization and forward momentum tended magically to increase everyone's income. Such are the manifold benefits of good communication protocol. When you hire representation, whether in the fields of law, accountancy, marketing, public relations, advertising, or any other field, don't accept anything less than a Brian Epstein. All too often, you won't hear from the agent, manager, or representative for long periods of time. Sometimes, the only communication occurs when you initiate it. This probably means that before the ink was dry on your agreement (if any), your agent or representative scurried off to locate and sign another client.

Likewise, don't be that kind of vendor yourself. Remember that each sale or client represents, on some level, a personal relationship. If you want to keep and grow your business, work like the Beatles and Brian Epstein: communicate, communicate, communicate!

17
Success

At some point in your journey, you will start hitting and exceeding your goals. Perhaps, if you're lucky, you will realize that you're the best at what you do. Now might be a good time to kick back, survey how far you have come, issue a round of congratulations, and take stock. Right? Wrong. Not even close.

Be on your guard. In any undertaking, the first winds of achievement can bring with them many perils: inflated egos, complacency, or, in some cases, even anger. Why did success take so long? Why wasn't it bigger, better, more thrilling? Is *this* what I've been working so hard for?

If there is one recurring idea or pattern of events in the career of the Beatles, it is that each success brings with it a new and even wider horizon for success. It is perhaps the best thing about success: the new markets, the new products, the new energy it calls into being. It's common to all world-beating enterprises, be they Beatles or Starbucks.

The Beatles' first single, "Love Me Do," recorded in 1962, had done well, if not spectacularly well, reaching the Top 20 on the British charts. Emboldened, on February 11, 1963, George Martin had taken them into the studio for a marathon 14-hour session to record their first album, *Please, Please Me.*

With the release of the album, the Beatles were soon awarded their first number-one record in England. Their bookings and pay increased, the venues and crowds began to grow in size, and television opportunities began to surface. The BBC was playing their music on the radio, even giving them their own live show for a time, called *Pop Go the Beatles.* They had finally made it to the very top of the English showbiz heap.

During this time, the Beatles did not rest on their laurels. In addition to their steady diet of personal appearances and TV and radio work, they were relentlessly accessible to any reporter, with any print publication, regardless of its circulation or lack thereof. Since thousands of fans were hungry for any information that they could find on the Beatles, the boys' exertions contributed greatly to the initial success of many of the newer publications. As the saying goes, a rising tide lifts all boats. In their success, the Beatles always bred more success.

With maturity beyond their years, the Beatles seized every day as if it were their last. And they began to set their sights on a conquest that no other British recording artist had ever attempted: the sprawling vastness of America, Britain's rebellious, uptight step-child. The British Invasion was about to begin.

After the first wave of success, new sales and marketing opportunities—even opportunities to grow through acquisition—may present themselves to you. So don't kick back and become one of the beautiful people. Not just yet. Instead, you must work even more diligently and intelligently to maintain momentum and move forward. You have conquered your Britain. Now go find your America.

18

Being Overlooked

What do you do when you have a proven winner and people still won't buy it, even though you *know* it's better than what they've got now? Do you keep on trying to cram it down their throats, or do you go back to the drawing board and come back with something new and even better? If you've been paying attention so far, I think you know the answer.

The Beatles had conquered the British Isles and had enjoyed success in other parts of Europe—in their familiar haunts in Germany, and in France as well. Soon enough, Spain and Portugal would be familiar with *Los Beatles* and *Os Beatles,* respectively. However, neither George Martin nor Brian Epstein could persuade Capitol records, the American EMI affiliate, to give the Beatles a chance. First, the executives at Capitol refused "Love Me Do." Even with the success of "Please, Please Me," a number-one album in Britain, they refused to issue the album or any of its accompanying singles. This rejection came as a great disappointment to the Beatles, and to their manager and producer. They were the most successful act that Britain had witnessed in years—perhaps ever. Could the American audience really be *that* different?

Martin and Epstein could have easily given in and accepted as fact that these Americans at Capitol knew more about their market, and that America was not ready or willing to accept the Beatles. However, the Beatles had too much cussed self-belief to give up on their audacious plan to conquer America. Martin, ever the pragmatist, leased the orphan titles to smaller, independent American record labels like Vee-Jay. And when they entered the studio and performed their latest composition, "I Want to Hold Your Hand," George Martin knew they had an absolute smash record. Following the recording of the song, he sent it to Capitol and later said, "I knew they couldn't turn that one down." They didn't. After one solid year of attempts to convince the American label that the Beatles were worthy of having a record released in the United States, the Beatles scored their first U.S. number-one hit on Capitol records.

The most important lesson here is not simple perseverance, though that *is* important. The approach was key. They did not continue to pitch Capitol the same product that they had already rejected. Instead, Martin contacted Capitol only when he had something new and improved. Apple Computer used a similar strategy to great effect. Never able to penetrate the corporate computer market like IBM and Microsoft in the 1980s, Apple could easily have gone the way of the Tandy microcomputer or the Commodore 64. Instead, Apple established preeminence in the educational markets and catered to the needs of creative professionals in the graphic arts and music. Along the way, they devised and established important industry standards like the use of a graphical user interface (GUI), as opposed to the "green screen." (Remember those?) In recent years, the development of iTunes, the iPod, and the iPhone—new, exciting products—have helped establish Apple as a ubiquitous presence in the majority of American homes and businesses.

You don't have a right to expect a perfectly rational response from your customers or prospective customers, even when what you're offering is clearly better than what they have now. Perhaps it is wiser to expect the opposite! Remember that even when the customer is wrong, the customer is always right. You can't force them to like you, or to buy what you are selling. Do as the Beatles did, and as Apple Computer did. Seek alternative opportunities and keep trying until you're ready to knock their socks off.

19
Humor

Why do you watch the Super Bowl? Many of you, I'm sure, would say it is because you love football. (In 2005, if you're a Beatles fan, you might have said that it was to see Sir Paul McCartney's rousing half-time show.) But a significant number of you might admit that the most entertaining part of the Super Bowl broadcast is the premiere of dozens of funny advertisements for big-dollar brands like Coke, Pepsi, Budweiser, Ford, and Toyota, as well as by numerous upstart companies or brands looking to make a big splash and create instant public awareness. Humor has always been a key element of effective sales, and probably always will be.

When the Beatles met the press in America, the media did not know what to expect. The fans had bought in, but the media of the day held to mainstream standards. The Beatles' humor won them over. The same humor that had pulled the band through the dreary days in Hamburg, the freezing trips throughout England, that had endeared them to Brian Epstein and George Martin, and to the English press, won over America. Upon landing in New York, they faced hundreds in attendance at their first press conference and handled it with unexpected wit and aplomb. In the first United States interview, the following exchanges took place.

> Question: How were you able to achieve this success?
> Beatles: We don't really know. If we did, we'd form another group and be managers.
>
> Question: Will you sing something?
> Lennon: We need money first.
>
> Question: Do you hope to get a haircut while you're visiting our country?
> Harrison: I had one yesterday.
> Ringo: You should have seen him the day before.

At work here was not just their undeniable facility with words, but also their unique delivery. Being from Liverpool, the Beatles all to one degree or another spoke in the accent of the area, known as *scouse*. (Scouse actually varied from neighborhood to neighborhood; George had more scouse in his speech than the others, especially John, who was brought up by his Aunt Mimi very deliberately *not* to speak scouse.) The Beatles learned early in the game that answering questions in a distinctly Liverpudlian manner, replete with exaggerated scouse, endeared them to the press and made their answers seem even funnier.

Humor—particularly humor rooted in who you are—can pull a person or a business through tough times, and make the good times better. It can knock a critic or a negative reporter off his game. It cements friendship, befriends the neutral, and neutralizes the enemy.

Keep 'em laughing—especially if you, like the Beatles, are offering something new or different that might be considered hard to understand, or even vaguely threatening. If you can use humor effectively in these circumstances, the chances are greater that you'll be laughing, too. All the way to the bank.

20
Paying the Price of Fame

Do you know what you will give up to achieve your success? And when the bill comes, are you willing and able to pay the tab without resentment? Because from here on out, it's going to cost you. Big. If this sounds a little scary, it should. It's my duty here to try to scare you. If I can scare you, it's time to put the book down and enjoy the fruits of what you have already achieved. Be happy with your lot in life. Spend time with your friends and family. If I can't scare you, read on. But don't say I didn't warn you.

By the middle of 1963, the Beatles had made the grade. They were internationally famous. They were selling millions of records and millions of dollars of Beatles merchandise, even if they were not seeing much of the money themselves (more on this in chapters 24 and 25). They were media darlings throughout the world, and had been signed up for a major motion picture by United Artists. This was all to the good and largely according to their plan.

Their fame posed certain challenges, however. They could no longer travel alone down the streets of the cities in which they toured. In fact, they were frequently in very real danger of being trampled or dismembered by hysterical fans on the way to and from of their concerts and hotels.

"So what?" you might think. "Poor Beatles, dealing with their runaway success. I should have such problems!" But complete lack of privacy and incessant hard work, not to mention fearing for life and limb night after night, had real psychological costs for the Beatles. Both Lennon and Harrison, to some degree, would directly or indirectly wonder in public whether the trade-off had been worth it.

If you want Beatle-style success in your business, your life will be defined as much by what you sacrifice as by what you achieve. How many extra hours you're willing to put in. How much you're willing to travel or otherwise spend time away from your family. How much you're willing to gamble, leveraging your personal assets and the assets of your family and business, in pursuit of the dream.

If and when such success comes, it creates enormous pressure. Ego—and its dark twin, insecurity—often become liabilities. Regardless of how powerful the skill or asset is that brought you to the forefront, you can rapidly lose the ability to contribute.

Incredible success creates risk and exposure to the dark forces in human nature. You cannot go on living as you did. You cannot go on living a "normal" life. In 1983, billionaire Alfred Henry Heineken, the Dutch beer magnate, was kidnapped and held for ransom for three weeks before being rescued by Dutch authorities—*after* the ransom had been paid. Heineken limited his public appearances thereafter, until his death in 2002. This dark side would eventually touch the Beatles. In 1999, George Harrison was stabbed by a crazed fan in his home, Friar Park located near Henley, even as he was trying to recover from an early bout with cancer. (Harrison would die of cancer in 2001.) And we all know what happened to John Lennon in 1980.

Be sure to take proactive steps to minimize or neutralize the intrusion of these dark forces into your success. Take the necessary steps to protect yourself and your loved ones. This may include security measures, but also adequate life and disability insurance to make sure that your family—and your business—can recover if something terrible does happen.

21
Record Every Thought

Have you ever wakened in the middle of the night with a great idea, perhaps a *really* great idea? Have you ever told yourself you'll remember it in the morning and fallen back to sleep? And had no earthly idea what it was in the morning light? Of course you have. Everybody has. Everybody, that is, but the Beatles.

One night, Paul McCartney awoke with a beautiful melody in his head, one that he felt he must have overheard somewhere. He dutifully arose, played it through enough times, and made enough notations, so that he would be able to remember it later. At that time, he gave the ditty the offhand title "Scrambled Eggs." After checking with everyone he knew over the next several weeks to make sure that the melody was, in fact, new and unique, McCartney began to craft more suitable lyrics. "Scrambled Eggs" became "Yesterday."

What if McCartney had simply told himself he'd remember the tune in the morning, and gone back to sleep? Or what if, convinced he was unconsciously plagiarizing somebody else, he had neglected to research whether the melody really was his own and worth pursuing? A fortune would have been lost—that's for sure. In the United States alone, "Yesterday" sold millions of singles and albums and has been played on the radio millions and millions of times and counting. It eventually spawned more than 3,000 commercially released "cover versions" by other artists.

All of the Beatles associates' from the early years have stated that John and Paul were constantly writing. They would write on napkins, in notebooks, on scraps of paper found on the floor, their hands, arms, anywhere. (Unfortunately, many of these early notes have been lost.) When they had attained some success, they bought tape recorders for their homes, so that they need never miss an opportunity to document a new song idea.

As your business grows, new experiences and opportunities will spawn ideas that may, in the words of the song, flow out like endless rain. Unfortunately, if not properly recorded, they may also slip away across the universe, never to be seen or heard from again. Record every thought. Don't let those golden ideas slip away into the ether. Keep a pad beside the bed. If you're traveling, call and leave yourself a voice mail. Tomorrow never knows the value that a small slip of an idea might have for you—and for the world.

22
Two of Us

Here's a little quiz. I'll give you a word, and you note the first thing that pops into your mind. Lennon. Jagger. Rodgers. Gilbert.

Have you ever heard of a *dyad?* If you thought, McCartney, Richard, Hammerstein (or perhaps Hart), and Sullivan, then you know what it is, even if you don't know the word itself. *Dyad* is a term of ancient origin that expresses the idea of two entities that must be considered as one. Marriages are dyadic, and many—if not most—extremely successful songwriters function dyadically. In addition to the above, the list goes on and on: Bjorn and Benny, Leiber and Stoller, Elton John and Bernie Taupin.

We've all heard the expression, "Two heads are better than one."

In creative endeavors (of which your business, make no mistake, is one) this axiom has special resonance. Effective partnerships can exist in many sizes, but some things are just meant to be done in twos. Common to dyadic partnerships is the sense that each partner has found some missing piece of the puzzle of his own identity in the other. At the very least, each has found a partner that can compensate for, or mask, his own shortcomings.

Shortly after John Lennon met Paul McCartney in 1957, he asked Paul to join his band, the Quarrymen. John had immediately seen that Paul possessed many talents that he himself lacked. He recognized that Paul was a better natural musician. At that point in time, John was not able to tune his own guitar, except in the fashion of a banjo: all the chords Lennon played on his guitar were banjo shapes. As the first order of business at their next meeting, Paul taught Lennon how to tune his guitar to standard or "Spanish" tuning.

In John, Paul saw the raw edge that he was missing. He could feel the strength and resolve in the youngster. He was aware of Lennon's keen wit, as he had noticed that when John did not know the words to the song he was singing, he would sing his own words— many of which seemed like improvements upon the original.

Lennon and McCartney were soon writing songs. Because Paul was left-handed, they would sit face-to-face and their guitars would line up symmetrically, as virtual mirror images of each other. Even down to this tiny physical detail, their differences inspired their mutual creativity. In this atmosphere of mutual inspiration and accountability, they created the bones of well over a hundred songs prior to the recording of their first album four years later.

At this point in your journey, you are probably well aware of your own weaknesses. There are things you are unable, or unwilling, to do on your own. The things you never seem to get to, that you know are important. Perhaps you are one of the cursed few who feel that they have to do everything themselves. Perhaps, if you are brutally honest, you will admit to yourself that you want the credit for something that you should be entrusting to someone else.

If this seems like you, take a page out of the Lennon-McCartney songbook. They agreed to ascribe both names to their songs, regardless of which partner had more input, and share the income 50/50. Thus, even though McCartney wrote the sentimental "Yesterday" more or less completely on his own, he shared the royalties equally with John. John reciprocated with many of his own masterworks throughout the years.

If you or your business is stalled, and deep down you recognize some "old business," some old familiar flaw that is once again tripping you up, maybe you have been waiting for someone to perform with. Perhaps it is time to find the other half of your business dyad. You may be tempted to enlarge the group beyond two, but chances are you already have one person in mind, someone with whom you have always been *simpatico*. Begin there, and discipline yourself to stay there for a while. You may be surprised at the results.

23
Revenue Streams

As the Beatles' first American tour unfurled, it became apparent to all that they were more than a recording act, more than a rock and roll band. They were a *bona fide* commercial phenomenon—one that could even perceptibly affect Britain's trade balance.

So what about the money, you may be asking? Surely the Beatles themselves were raking it in by this time. Actually, for all the money that swirled around the Beatles, they—at least initially—kept precious little of it. It took them a lifetime to amass the fortunes that the two surviving Beatles and the heirs of Lennon and Harrison enjoy today.

If you crave Beatle-level success, don't imagine that you will achieve instant wealth. For the Beatles, there were no short-cuts. They worked hard and maximized the number of revenue streams that their work generated. Records, performances, radio, TV, movies, sheet music, merchandising—from the simple acts of writing a few songs and getting up onstage to sing, there emerged at least half a dozen revenue streams or more, depending on how you count. Each one of these revenue streams was crucial in its own way.

All four Beatles earned so-called *mechanical* royalties from the sale of their records (as recording artists, not as writers or publishers). These were important, because once the Beatles stopped performing, this became George and Ringo's primary source of Beatle income. Every time there is a Beatle re-issue, or a new format such as the CD is developed, a huge windfall arrives for Ringo and Paul and for the estates of Lennon and Harrison. Even Pete Best reaped a substantial fortune from the first volume of the *Anthology,* released in 1995—thirty-three years after he was sacked from the band! (He is credited as a performer—a member of the Beatles—on eleven tracks.)

Early on, royalty income would have been a slow trickle. It's a good thing they earned substantial fees from live performances, as well as for appearances on TV and radio broadcasts. They all received ready money from licensed Beatles merchandise, and eventually from their work as actors in movies.

Lennon and McCartney, as composers, had numerous additional medium-term and long-term revenue streams. Besides a second set of mechanical royalties (from writing and publishing) from the sale of Beatle records, they earned mechanical licensing fees from the sale of records of other artists who recorded their songs (recall that "Yesterday" has enjoyed 3,000 "cover" versions over the years). Anytime their songs were played or performed on the radio, by themselves or by others, Lennon and McCartney received *performance* royalties as well. Sheet music for popular songs also generates cash for composers. And although it is rare, synchronization rights for the use of Beatle music on TV or in the movies was also a source of income for John and Paul. Maybe you think figuring Social Security and Medicare taxes is a hassle. Try figuring out a Beatle paycheck.

Like John and Paul, you may be entitled to more than one type of compensation for your product or service—if you are alert to exploit it. If you have a successful service business, perhaps it is time to create a local or regional franchise—these can serve as "cover" versions of your services and they can generate income for you while you are sleeping or on vacation. This is one of the most crucial landmarks in the life of an entrepreneur—when her income is no longer directly tied to the number of hours she puts in.

If you have a successful product, think of it like a song. The Beatles, in their way, were akin to an OEM supplier, a manufacturer of products to be sold under multiple retail labels. Their songs—whether the real thing, or knockoffs by other artists—were eventually built into larger vehicles like films and TV programs. In this way, they were introduced to larger and different markets than they could reach on their own. (See chapter 29 for an illustration of the dramatic effect their debut on America's *Ed Sullivan Show* had on their fortunes.)

What is your "song"? And how many different ways can you think of to get paid for it?

24
Financial Planning

Are you a financial planner, or a financial survivor? The Beatles, for most of their careers, were the latter. Before success came, they had managed to buy adequate instruments and new leather clothing. They ate reasonably well, consumed considerable amounts of alcohol, and even managed to stay enlivened through the use of (legal) pep pills in the Hamburg days. Needless to say, none of them had a retirement fund, a children's college fund, or even an emergency fund. (Lennon and Best even attempted a mugging when cash ran short in Hamburg.)

After success came, there was no more need to mug drunken sailors, but being a Beatle was still a hand-to-mouth affair throughout most of the 1960s. Part of the problem was inadequate representation. For all his other virtues, Brian Epstein was grossly inexperienced in negotiating licensing, merchandising, publishing, and recording contracts. He had nonetheless attempted to negotiate these contracts without consulting professionals. Unbeknownst to his mop-topped clients, he was overprotective of his relationship with them. Not only was he fearful that outside counsel might exploit the Beatles—even worse, if they did too well for the boys, they might replace *him* in the Beatles' affection. The results were, in a word, disastrous. In the Beatles' primary American merchandising deal, the principals were willing to take 10 percent, yet Brian made the proposal backward, giving the Beatles 10 and the merchandisers 90!

This kind of arrangement might have been easier to survive had the Beatles' bread-and-butter deals in recording and music publishing been better. However, George Martin had signed the Beatles to an unusually stingy contract, with only a penny royalty for every two-sided single record sold. Of this one English penny, Brian Epstein and NEMS took 25 percent off the top, leaving the Beatles with three-quarters of a penny, or three "farthings," to split four ways. So, for every *million* records sold, the Beatles took home just 7,500 pounds or 1,875 pounds apiece. And this sum was their before-tax income. (For a discussion of the punitive English taxes that further damaged the Beatles' finances, see the next chapter.)

The result? Though there were worldwide tours, movies, records, television appearances, and hundreds of licensed products including lunchboxes, posters, photographs, notebooks, trading cards, boots, wigs, and dolls—within three years, the Beatles would be on the verge of bankruptcy.

So how is it that the two surviving Beatles, and the estates of Lennon and Harrison, are now worth untold millions (and, in McCartney's case, about a billion)? It should be noted that this was largely the result of several contract renegotiations, nearly forty years of solo work, residual income from continued sales of the Beatles catalog, and some canny investments. If all four men were living, they would be at or approaching retirement age as the principals of a very successful cottage industry, such as the Harry Potter books or the Cabbage Patch dolls. In that sense, there is nothing remarkable about their current wealth. (J. K. Rowling is worth more than Paul McCartney, and she is in her early 40s.)

Things turned out O.K. for the Beatles, to be sure, but consider this: every million dollars that slipped through their fingers in 1964, would have been worth about $64 million in 2006. (This assumes about a 10 percent return per year.) Such is the power of compound interest over time. Though it is hard to figure how much exactly the Beatles left on the table in the 1960s, a figure of $15 or $16 million is a conservative estimate. That sum, conservatively invested, would be worth roughly another *billion* dollars today. There is no substitute for exploiting the time value of money!

This is not to take the Beatles to task. Financial planning and preparing for retirement are disciplines that eluded a large percentage of the Beatles-era population, including the Beatles themselves. They were too busy making music to pay attention, or seek adequate representation to make sure that their financial interests were being well managed. And even if they had been paying attention, it might not have helped. As Joey Molland of Badfinger has said, discussing his band's contractual troubles, "Young people shouldn't try to be smart. They should hire lawyers to be smart for them."

Make this part of the business plan from the very beginning. Remember the astronomical figures lost to the Beatles and don't let dollars slip through your grasp. If you are too busy to chase them down, hire someone—be it a lawyer or an accountant—who can. Remember that phantom billion the Beatles lost. Start now!

25
Taxman

In their early years, the boys worked in nightclubs and were paid in cash. The Beatles knew little about income taxes. However, they were quick studies. They had to be. At one point in their careers, they were paid in cash in small bags. They had no idea of their worth or their liabilities. In fact, Brian had made so many bad deals that he was embarrassed to explain to them the details of their financial situation.

As their income finally, against all odds, increased, the Beatles fell victim to the English "super tax" on the wealthy. By the end of their existence as Beatles, they were only retaining a tiny percentage—in the single digits—of their income. Harrison's song "Taxman" was not an exaggeration by any means.

This may seem fanciful or look like a misprint, but it is not. England has had a heavy hand with taxes. (After all, the American Revolution began as a tax revolt.) The Beatles were not about to start their own country, however much the notion might have appealed to their well-established utopian impulses. With proper advice and representation, however, they could have avoided at least part of this crushing tax liability through legal solutions such as the creation of off-shore corporations or by establishing residency in other countries during peak earning periods (as the Rolling Stones later did).

The most effective tax write-off the Beatles ever created was Apple. This record company, publishing company, retail boutique, and vehicle for Beatle whimsy steadily bled them of all their cash reserves in the late 1960s. (More on this starting in chapter 61.) However, this was far from a resounding success, even as a tax strategy. Each Beatle would continue to be plagued by large tax bills—some in the millions of pounds—well into the 1970s. In the end, the withering English taxes may have caused as much as anything else the gradual disenchantment that the Beatles began to feel with their common enterprise. It affected their willingness to get out of bed and Beatle, which, as we have seen, was an all-encompassing commitment.

While you may never face the onerous tax structure that the Beatles did, you should still consider the tax benefits and liabilities of your proposed business structure, industry, and location at the outset. Just as many an entertainer has run into tax problems through inattention or trust in unscrupulous or incompetent representation, so too has many an entrepreneur run into serious difficulty by failing to budget adequately, on a quarterly basis, for tax payments.

Each industry has its unique tax deductions, credits, and shelters. You should explore these with experts in the field of taxation. The tax codes are complicated beasts that attempt to devour all and are understood by few. Find one of the few. And do it early, to avoid the Beatle dilemma of generating enormous sums of money for everyone but yourself.

26
Enjoying the Ride

Do you believe that getting there is half the fun? On the road to Beatle-size greatness, you should realize that getting there may well be half the fun, all the fun, or no fun at all. The choice is largely up to you, and it should be a purposeful one. But there will be some factors that are out of your control. Reviewing chapters 1 and 2 may be a good idea at this juncture. It may help you stay in touch with the essentials—who you are and what your dream is— as other factors intrude (as they inevitably will).

For the Beatles, "getting there" began in 1960 as they left for Hamburg in the van of their then-manager, Alan Williams. The ride continued through 1961 and 1962 in Neil Aspinall's van, as they drove all over Britain, with or without a windshield. At this point, the Beatles still lived in a world of interesting and expanding horizons. The ride was still fun.

But by 1964-65, they had hit the "glass ceiling" of the pop world. When the Beatles eventually became the first group to play in stadiums, it became clear that there was nowhere to go but down as a live act. There simply were no larger venues available on the planet. They were flying all over the world in chartered jets (their overhead had increased dramatically). At each stop, they were whisked from the plane into limos in a motorcade, placed behind microphones in front of naïve, abrasive members of the media, and asked about their hair and their girlfriends ad nauseam. Next they were driven to their hotel where they were held hostage until they could be driven to the auditorium or stadium. There, they would perform a 30-minute concert, rendered inaudible by the screaming masses in attendance. Finally, they were shoved into the limos among screaming, pressing, crushing fans and deposited back in their hotel rooms. Once in their rooms, they answered fan mail, wrote songs, and held meetings to discuss the following day. But the fun was gone.

In 1960, John and Ringo were twenty, Paul was eighteen, and George was seventeen. They were unknown even in their own hometown. In 1964, they were the most famous people in the world. The journey from the Woolton Fete at St. Peter's Church in Liverpool where John and his Quarrymen played to a smattering of Liverpudlians to the 56,400 fans at Shea Stadium in New York City had been a brief one, yet they had packed a lifetime of experience into it.

The fame and success was the goal that pulled them through the dankness and darkness of the Bambi Kino in Hamburg, the sweltering heat of the Cavern, and the frozen van rides across Britain. When the group was feeling low in the early days, John Lennon invented a ritual cheer to defeat the sadness and gloom. He would shout in an American accent, "Where're we goin' fellas?" In unison, the others would shout "to the top, Johnny, to the top!" Lennon would then repeat his question, and the correct response was "To the Toppermost of the Poppermost!" That's where they went, but by and large they did not enjoy the journey as much as they might have. Gradually, they would retreat to the relative quiet of the recording studio.

The Beatles never saw what hit them. You can avoid this fate by going in with your eyes open. As your business starts its ascent to the toppermost, realize the ride has begun. Remember that with all its stresses and problems, it may well be the most exciting, profitable, and storied part of your life. Savor it. Because once you get where you're going, it will be too late to enjoy the ride.

27

Off the Record

Have you ever played the Telephone game? You know the one: everybody sits in a circle or around a table and someone whispers in the ear of his neighbor. The secret thought is whispered from person to person around the circle. If there are several people, by the time it comes back around to its originator, it is usually changed beyond recognition. Here's a question: Would you like your reputation to hinge upon a big game of Telephone? No? That's too bad, *because it does*.

As a business attains a higher level of success, the leaders of that business may become revered in the community and the industry. The behavior of these individuals is monitored by their competitors, their peers, and their followers. If they stumble, whether in business or in their personal affairs, the business gossip network can be just as far-reaching and thorough with its dissemination of information as any media outlet. Worse, the information will be subject to even less verification than it is in the media.

As fame overcame them, the Beatles learned that they had to be guarded every time they were in the presence of anyone other than their inner circle. The world was starved for every morsel that the media could report about them, especially about their personal relationship with the women in their lives. They were photographed each time they left the confines of their homes, hotel rooms, or the recording studio. The genesis of the intrusive and even dangerous modern *paparazzi* took place largely in the free-wheeling Beatle era. Some members of the press actually scavenged through their garbage in efforts to find information. In such a predatory environment, many a Beatle and Beatle associate came to regret sharing something in confidence or "off the record."

Remember the old wartime admonition: loose lips sink ships. Keep your thoughts about your business within the inner circle. And remember that your personal life is not out of bounds, nor is it unrelated to the continued success of the business.

28
The Mysterious B7

One of the reasons that the Beatles' music seemed so fresh and unique was that it *was* fresh and unique. In the early days, they were always working to expand their musical abilities. The story goes that the teenaged John, Paul, and George heard of a person on the other side of Liverpool who had learned a chord they didn't know—the B7. They hurried over to that person—taking their guitars with them on the bus—to learn that new chord.

Both Lennon and McCartney spoke later of anxiously awaiting the boats coming into the port at Liverpool with the newest American records. They would learn the songs and add them to their repertoire. They were also familiar with the repertoire of Tin Pan Alley and of the English music hall. When they began to write songs, the chords and chord progressions they learned from these sources became the database, the mental background music, they would use to construct their own songs. Such dedication paid off. Though the exact numbers differ according to the source, it is generally acknowledged that the Beatles used more chords in their songs—even their early songs—than the standard three or four chords that had been used in rock and roll up to that time.

Some forty years later, one of us (Richard) decided to attempt to learn Beatles songs on the guitar in order to entertain himself and maybe gain some insight into what these four lads from Liverpool were all about. He had no interest in theory or notation. He wanted to learn to play a few songs exactly as the Beatles had on the records. Living in Nashville, he was fortunate to be able to hire Gary Talley, guitar player for the Box Tops, a band that had hits in the 1960s with "The Letter" and "Cry Like a Baby."

Gary had Richard bring in the CDs that included the songs he wanted to learn and he would listen along, pick a note or two, rewind, pick another note, try a chord, and soon be playing right along. One of the first songs Richard asked to be taught was "I Want to Hold Your Hand." He listened, remarked that John was playing power chords on the opening C and D chords. Then he began to walk him through the first four measures. "O.K. Here goes. G on the *Oh yeah I'll tell some,* now switch, go a D on *thing.*" Then he listened intently, rewound the CD, and said, "Right, it's an Em for *I think you'll under . . .* then it's a, um." He rewound the CD. "Let's see." He listened, a wrinkle creasing his forehead. He tried a few chords. Then he hit it and smiled. "That's weird. They played a B7."

The Beatles were always hungry for knowledge. And when they gained it, they applied it in unusual, unexpected ways that still surprise and give us pleasure today. In fact, the plot thickens. Because of the way that the Beatles framed and articulated the chord and melody, some musicologists hear the chord in question as a B minor or B minor seventh chord, which calls attention to an interesting fact: from their omission or understatement of the crucial third note in the chord, the Beatles created a vacuum, a sort of instability in the key center of the music. This instability is interesting and pleasing to the listener. (Later in the song, in the eighth measure of each verse, an unequivocal B7 does appear, and the third is stated or clearly implied as a major interval.)

That the work of these four men barely in their 20s could inspire such a lasting mystery (or at least controversy) among the learned, whether intentionally or not, is a testament to that unique talent they possessed. It would be nonetheless interesting to hear Paul McCartney's verdict on the name of the chord. Sir Paul? (For the aspiring or practicing guitarist, articulate a B, F sharp, and A on the lower strings of the guitar and you can't go wrong.)

The same is possible in any line of business, including yours. Most likely, you and your competitors probably learned your B7 a long time ago. (If not, get on the bus and go learn it!) Right now, you and your competitors are probably using the B7 in all the conventional ways—doing the same old song and dance. What is your B7? Re-examine it. Add something. Leave something out. Find some new setting or context. Give it new life. Don't be afraid to add a little instability, a little mystery, a little magic—as John and Paul did.

29

No Pain, No Gain

No pain, no gain. When you're working out, if you're not a little sore afterward, you're not building muscle. You actually must stretch the muscle, damaging and tearing it a little bit, in order for it to rebuild itself a little bigger and stronger for the next workout.

Likewise, in business, if you are in your comfort zone, you are not going to grow your capabilities. You're just repeating yourself. Only when you are stretched to your limit—fraying at the edges—will you learn and master the skills necessary to get to the next level.

For the Beatles, there was plenty of pain in the early and mid-1960s. Following the sleep-deprived tours of the United Kingdom,

Paris, and Hamburg in 1963, and the recording and release of their first international hits "I Want to Hold Your Hand" and "She Loves You," the Beatles opened 1964 in Paris—then went on to New York and Miami for three episodes of the *Ed Sullivan Show*, the first of which aired on February 9, 1964.

After rehearsals and sound checks, the Beatles visited the control room to instruct the engineers on how their sound should be broadcast to the viewers. They ensured that the perfect mix of instruments and vocals were audible over the screaming studio audience. Reporters and fans alike were amazed that the Beatles were constantly rehearsing for the shows, and for their upcoming tour of the United States.

The Beatles did all this work for a fee of $3,500 per show. There are those who think that Brian Epstein could have—should have—demanded more money. But really, they could have paid *Sullivan* $3,500 and Epstein's strategy would still have been brilliant. Unlike England, which had the BBC, the American market was highly regional and variegated. But more than *73 million* Americans were glued to their television sets for the Sullivan show. The suits, the boots, the hair, the songs, the stances of the Beatles, along with their head waving, smiling, and stamping are still imitated more than forty years later. In those three weeks, the capstone of years of hard work, and thanks to Epstein's brilliant strategy, the Beatles stole the hearts and ears of America. (And if Epstein had turned down the booking by disputing a few thousand dollars? Nothing! None of it would ever have happened.) No pain, no gain.

The relentless pace continued as the U.S. visit ended later that month. The Beatles began the filming of their first feature film, *A Hard Day's Night,* later that month. During the shooting of the movie, they wrote and recorded the entire soundtrack album, including the hits "A Hard Day's Night," "I Should Have Known Better," "Can't Buy Me Love," "And I Love Her," "If I Fell," and "You Can't Do That," among others. Many of these classic songs were written in single sittings under the stress and pressures of deadlines. No pain, no gain.

The album and the movie were released in the summer of 1964. Then back on the road for tours all over the world. Then into the studio to record *Beatles For Sale* for a November (pre-Christmas) release. This album included Lennon-McCartney songs such as "I'm a Loser," "Eight Days a Week," "I'll Follow the Sun," and "I Don't Want to Spoil the Party," along with several other originals that were written on movie sets, in hotel rooms, in dressing rooms, and on airplanes.

This routine of relentless touring and recording roughly two albums a year continued for all of 1963, 1964, 1965, and most of 1966. These were the Beatle undergraduate years. And it was indeed a rigorous course of study, more all-consuming than engineering at MIT or pre-med at Harvard.

Do you feel like you're on a treadmill right now? Are you sore with the effort of maintaining your current pace of activity? Good. Chances are, with a little examination, you will discover certain milestones—your Sullivan show, your first feature film—that mark inexorable progress along a course of study for still greater things to come. The Beatles did. As it turns out, they were about to graduate, with high honors.

No pain, no gain.

30
Rest and Recovery

In the last chapter, we explored the concept of no pain, no gain. Once you have picked the direction of your dream, exceptionally hard work and total involvement is the best guarantor of exceptional success. However, there is an important caveat here, and it underscores an important turning point in the career of the Beatles and in this book. Although you must tear and stretch muscle, a period of rest and recovery is equally important. Without such intermittent periods of rest and recovery, the muscle cannot rebuild itself properly. Your capabilities cannot grow. When you return to the task at hand, you will still be sore, still be tired, from the last exertions.

The Beatles took brief vacations during their four-year journey to the top. But they never had a sufficient period of rest and recovery to truly regain their equilibrium and comfortably exercise the enhanced capabilities and enlarged possibilities that all of their hard work had won for them. The Beatles were beat, and the strain was starting to show in their performances. When they toured Japan, where polite audiences did not scream and the music was clearly audible, elaborate harmony numbers like "Nowhere Man" dissolved into near train wrecks. Their lush, elaborate studio vocal arrangements simply could not be effectively reproduced under the hectic and rigorous travel conditions that prevailed on a Beatles tour.

In 1966, to the dismay of their manager and the world in general, the Beatles decided to stop touring. The big question in everyone's mind was whether a recording act could sell records without making personal appearances. In fact, it wasn't really a question; most people assumed—based on precedent—that the Beatles were effectively finished. Once again, the world had underestimated John Lennon and his partners—the little band from Liverpool that *could*.

There will come a time when you feel that you and your business have grown stale. In reality, they are probably as good as before. This perception is no more than your tired body, mind, and soul urging you to take a break. You'll think about throwing in the towel, and start wondering what's next. Maybe you will start fantasizing about the wonders of retirement. Don't do it! Not yet! You have more to give . . .

Do what the Beatles did instead. Chapters 31 and 32 will describe the beneficial effects of taking a little inspiration from the competition, and of putting a little leisure time to good use. In fact, a well-timed break of even a couple of weeks—a mini-sabbatical—may be just the period of rest and recovery that you need to re-boot your system with all the software upgrades that your experiences to date have downloaded automatically into your subconscious. When you come back, you will be walking on hot coals with a smile and levitating small objects at will. O.K., maybe that's an exaggeration—but give your mind and body time to catch up with you. I guarantee that you won't be sorry you did.

31
Swimming with the Sharks

When you're at the top, how do you keep moving? After all, entrepreneurs and their businesses are like sharks— they've got to keep moving, or die.

The Beatles faced up to this challenge. They had played the largest venues in the world. There was no mountain remaining to be scaled in the live performance arena. And though they were not averse to using outside musicians on their records (starting with the string quartet on "Yesterday"), they did not want to do this in their live show, preferring to maintain the integrity of their four-man brand. Unlike the touring acts of later years, it would have horrified the Beatles to add percussionists, extra guitarists, keyboardists, or backup vocalists in order to help ease their musical workload and create visual interest.

Unlike the Stones or the Who, there was no dancing front man or jumping, high-kicking, wind-milling guitarist. The Beatles' showmanship was defined by their fine harmony singing—a point of pride that tended to root them in front of their microphones. Though they nonetheless managed to connect with their audience by shaking their heads, stamping their feet, winking, and smiling, they had reached their peak as live performers and felt they were going over the same old ground or—worse—losing ground. They all admitted that they did not want to be singing "She Loves You" for the rest of their lives. Something in them demanded to move forward, and not rest on their laurels. After they rested and recuperated, they were ready to swim with the sharks. To battle stagnation, they retreated into the studio to place a greater emphasis on writing and recording new music.

As they did so, they drew inspiration from the competition, Bob Dylan in particular. All of the Beatles had great respect for Dylan. John constantly referred to "You've Got to Hide Your Love Away" and "I'm a Loser" as "Lennon doing Dylan." The others were impressed, as well. (George professed a lifelong fanship and later worked with Dylan in the Traveling Wilburys.)

A keen awareness of their market and their competition helped snap the Beatles from the doldrums of stagnation. Assimilating the achievements of one's competition in ways that benefit one's own business—as the Beatles did with Dylan—is very advanced entrepreneurial behavior. Are you ready to "throw down" in this inward-outward tussle? Are you ready to commit—again? Then look around you. What are your competitors doing right? How does it inspire you? How does it frighten you? Cherish that fear—it's telling you where you need to go next.

32
Lifelong Learning

During this first, strenuous phase of building your business, it is likely that even your leisure activities will be directed in channels that are related to your business. This may be out of sheer enthusiasm, or out of a sense of obligation, as opportunities arise based on your success that you realize you "ought" to take advantage of.

You will be aided greatly in this journey if you commit yourself to the principle of lifelong learning. Key contributors typically will devote their time to acquiring, absorbing, and adapting knowledge in related (or even unrelated) fields. But you can derive benefits from more passive approaches as well, even watching TV. Successful, driven individuals usually can't help themselves.

It certainly was this way with the Beatles. Following the making of their second full-length film, George began to devote himself to the sitar and Indian music. Paul became a vigorous student and patron of all of the arts—visual, musical, performing, and literary. He attended concerts and plays, read books and poetry, and bought every new album he could get his hands on. He became particularly interested in the Beach Boys, as Brian Wilson was also emerging as something of a pop genius in his harmonies and arrangements. John became virtually consumed by Bob Dylan's works and would listen for hours on end. The Beatles had met Dylan on their first U.S. tour. John and Dylan had established a friendship, and Dylan would usually visit Lennon on his tours of England.

When they returned to the studio to create the *Revolver* album, they brought materials influenced by their newfound information. McCartney brought an urge to experiment based on his avant-garde art experiences and the challenge being laid down by competitors such as Brian Wilson. Lennon brought a decidedly Dylanesque sense of wordplay to bear. Harrison gilded the lily with exotic Indian instrumental flourishes on several new tracks.

Without their individual excursions into the unknown, the shape of the Beatles' career would have been markedly different. They would *not* have grown and evolved as they did, thereby establishing themselves as arguably the greatest musical group in history. These fresh new influences were not forced—they flowed logically out of the principals' curiosity and natural bent for learning new things.

Commit yourself to lifelong learning—always think about what's next. Your business will thank you.

33

The Corporate Connection

So far so good, right? Once again, the undeniable talent and unbridled originality of a small cadre of four triumph over all obstacles, right? Well, sort of. Read on.

For the album that was to become *Revolver,* Paul contributed the now classic "Eleanor Rigby," "Here, There, and Everywhere," and the Motown-inspired "Got to Get You into My Life," a song that included a masterfully arranged horn section. George Harrison contributed the Indian inspired "Love To You" and the wonderfully crafted song "Taxman," as well as "I Want to Tell You." (The album became the first to contain three George Harrison originals.) John weighed in with the sardonic, autobiographical "She Said She Said" and "I'm Only Sleeping."

When the Beatles reconvened in the studio, producer George Martin had also brought a new engineer, Geoff Emerick, into the control room. The Beatles' engineer up to that point, Norman "Normal" Smith, had been promoted to the artist and repertoire (A & R) department of EMI, largely as a result of his success with the Beatles. This routine corporate promotion, and the changes that resulted, is a likely spot to consider the ways in which the staff, resources, and facilities of the EMI Corporation helped create and support the Beatles phenomenon. Emerick, working on the album that would become known as *Revolver,* helped change forever the manner in which pop songs, or any songs for that matter, were recorded.

For the Beatles, the studio had been evolving from a workaday environment into a sort of second home—or more accurately— a sort of gentlemen's club, where they could pursue their music with a sense of freedom, leisure, and experimentation. However, none of this would have been possible without the corporate background infrastructure, the steadily humming machine that EMI provided.

EMI's studio at Abbey Road (known now worldwide as "Abbey Road" studios, thanks largely to the Beatles) was a regimented facility, where small armies of engineers, tape operators, and technicians wore coats and ties and sometimes even laboratory coats whose color denoted the status and function of its wearer. The staff underwent rigorous technical training in all aspects of recording, from the placement of microphones in front of the sound source, to the "mixing" of multiple sounds into a pleasing and coherent whole, to the creation of the "master" copies of each record to use in the manufacturing process.

The EMI staff was even able to design, build, and maintain its own recording equipment—a fact which would figure heavily in the Beatles' story as they began to request more and more unusual sounds, some of which could not be achieved by then-existing equipment.

Emerick had risen through the EMI ranks quickly, and was young enough to have a healthy disregard for the "rules," a fact that endeared him to the Beatles. Emerick was not fazed when John Lennon told him that his voice should sound like the Dalai Lama singing from a mountaintop. Run the voice through a rotating speaker cabinet (normally used for an electric organ). Problem solved. He thought nothing of flipping the tape around and recording a guitar solo with the tape reversed, so that when the song is played forward, the guitar solo is played backward (this is a distinctive and now easily recognizable sound, in which each note fades in and ends with the "attack" of the plectrum). He was willing to cut a tape into little pieces, glue it all back together in random pieces, and add it to the final mix, if that was what the Beatles wanted. He was even willing to risk damaging EMI's precious equipment by placing microphones closer to loud sound sources than regulations permitted, resulting in an immediacy that had not been equaled to that time (and seldom since).

A maverick like Emerick was perfect for the moment, just as Smith had been perfect for the earlier, more traditional recordings. Neither one would have been available to the Beatles had they been on a smaller record label without its own studio. Though there were quality independent studios (such as Olympic), other talented engineers (such as Glyn Johns), and suitable arrangers (such as Mike Leander), EMI was the only one-stop shop for all three: Abbey Road, Geoff Emerick, and George Martin. This corporate brain trust was a unique advantage, one that the Beatles exploited to the fullest, even if they did not think of it in such terms!

After the Beatles made their magic music, still other facilities of EMI were responsible for overseeing the manufacture and distribution of the records. Examined in this light, the Beatles' recording work stands exposed as something of a corporate, even industrial enterprise, at the center of it all, the "talent" creating what only they could create. All around these absolutely essential contributors, a platoon of highly specialized staff and equipment were engaged in capturing, processing, and distributing the resulting product in large quantities. The Beatles' effect on the world would have been less far-reaching without EMI, no matter how high the quality of the raw material.

In your business, no matter how small or unconventional, understand the value of support structures and staff, and of a traditional corporate organization. People need to be immersed in the routines and procedures of your business, even if only to come up with something better. Remember EMI and Geoff Emerick. Something as bland as a routine promotion can change everything!

34
The Media

By this time, if your business is on track, the media has found you, whether you wanted to be found or not. Once they do, be careful. Bad things can happen with innocent comments. Often, the potentially disastrous results are caused by competent and well-meaning members of the media—and then there is the inflammatory, witch-hunting, unscrupulous minority that coexists alongside them. Remember the law of unintended consequences. Remember it, and respect it.

In the case of the Beatles, they had befriended a reporter named Maureen Cleave who wrote for the *Evening Standard*. Cleave had reported on the group since their early days and was a member of their inner circle as their popularity grew. After their triumphant return from the U.S., she interviewed the Beatles and was told by John Lennon that he felt that Christianity was losing its momentum, and that the Beatles were now more popular than Christ.

When Lennon spoke these words, he was perhaps lulled by his familiarity with the reporter and with the English audience who read her work. These remarks were not the focus of the article, merely asides. He was certainly not the first public figure across the pond to speculate on the decline of religion. The tenor of his comments would have been familiar to his intended audience, typifying as they did the self-consciously provocative undergraduate musings one might hear in any beatnik cafe, albeit layered with notes of personal bravado and self-congratulation.

The trouble began when the comments were repackaged in the United States—this time as the focus of an article. In some ways, America was as different from England as Japan. For better or worse, many American fans were not as phlegmatic about attacks on their religion and took umbrage at a twenty-something entertainer comparing himself favorably to the person Christianity worshiped as God incarnate. There were organized record burnings, and the Beatles themselves were even burned in effigy.

It's all too easy to blame the media or the American public for the flap, but really the culprit was Lennon. Millions of people the world over had been gracious enough to invite the Beatles into their homes—by way of buying records—to sing and to entertain them. Over time Lennon became a familiar and welcome figure in their homes, by his own design. His audience had every right to blanch as he then began to attack—or seemed to attack—their most strongly held spiritual beliefs. Of course, he was entitled to his opinions, but he should never have shared them with the press. Imagine (pun intended) if the CEO of McDonalds were to announce that the Big Mac was more popular than God among the children of today. Whether the statement is true or not, would that be a plus or a minus for the brand? Some things are best left unsaid.

Lennon eventually issued a half-hearted apology that was enough to placate most observers. However, the remark cost the Beatles a significant segment of their fan base forever. And quite needlessly! The sting of rejection seemed especially to hurt Lennon—for the rest of his career he would become increasingly emphatic in his efforts to prove how little being a Beatle had meant to him, anyway—a note of "sour grapes" that underlies the more traditional narrative of his growth away from the Beatles.

Once you are public property, be careful where and how you express your opinions. Remember that you *asked* to be in the game. Today, every person in every restaurant, retail outlet, subway— heck, anyone anywhere—is a potential member of the paparazzi by virtue of his cell phone. With the accessibility of the Internet and outlets such as youtube.com, the slightest indiscretion can garner worldwide coverage within the hour. During the 1960s, paparazzi were not so prevalent as they are today. With their cumbersome cameras and sound equipment, they were easily recognized and almost as easily avoided. Not so today. Repeat after me: the media is everyone, and everyone is the media.

Although you may think something you say is meaningless,

others may always remember it. Keep your mouth zipped, and talk to your public through—or at least with the assistance of—public relations professionals. Let that be the subject of the next chapter.

35
Public Relations

A company without a public relations component to its business plan will encounter difficulty with its branding, its image, and its message to the masses. The best way to learn how to work with the media is through a public relations firm. It is better for the media and it is better for the client.

Consider the Beatles. The verdict of history is that there is a clear arc of growing sophistication and accomplishment in the Beatles' music from 1962 to 1969. Paradoxically, however, their fan base began to fragment, and even shrink, by 1966. To be sure, the Beatles remained popular—hugely so. But it is indisputable that as the Beatles began to emancipate themselves from the restrictive but effective PR regime of Brian Epstein, they began to shed fans in large numbers without any help from others whatsoever.

There were many causes. Inevitably, changes in their music would leave behind some who preferred the earlier, simpler numbers. Increased competition from other English groups, as well as re-energized American musicians inspired by the Beatles (such as the Byrds), siphoned off fans. There were Lennon's statements regarding religion. There was an incident in Manila when the Beatles snubbed an invitation from Imelda Marcos to attend a reception at her palace. The masses turned against them and the band was forced to hide in laundry hampers with the dirty laundry to escape the country without injury. Later on, there would come Paul's decision to inform the media that the Beatles used LSD. Numerous Beatle drug busts and weddings took their toll. People became disenchanted or lost their personal interest in the once-cuddly moptops. With each PR gaffe, they lost market share. And these PR problems would continue to haunt them well into the 1970s, even possibly accounting for poor record sales for some of their solo efforts.

Prepare for the scrutiny. As your business succeeds, the spokespeople for your organization should receive media training for the print, radio, and television media.

36
Paradigms, Boxes, Fences, and the Like

The Beatles spent the summer of 1966 on tour in the U.S. Most of that time they were defending themselves against the "more popular than Jesus" statement, and avoiding being trampled. By that time, the hotel rooms, planes full of reporters, and shrieking fans were certainly more of a nuisance than a pleasurable experience.

As previously mentioned, in August 1966 the Beatles shocked the world when they made one of the most significant decisions in their career. The highest-grossing live act of all time (to that point) decided to discontinue personal appearances. No more concerts, no more tours. From now on, they would focus on writing and recording new songs. Effectively, the Beatles turned their back on one of their biggest revenue streams to focus on another core business. Or perhaps it would be more accurate to say that the Beatles chose to focus on product development, while closing a primary sales channel for that product. They would now be forced to rely exclusively on radio play and filmed appearances to sell their records to the world.

It was a bold move, one in which few could see the percentages. But it was not crazy. Aside from their personal fatigue and exhaustion, their high gross income was not translating into higher take-home pay, because their overhead had also increased dramatically. They were still committed to the group, so something in them demanded that they explore the only viable way forward—like commandos, they shot their way out of an untenable situation.

In your business, at some point you may see the need to make radical changes to your strategy. The world may call you crazy. Your associates and friends—some of whom may have a stake in the old ways of doing things—may try to dissuade you. If they can, then maybe you are crazy. But you know your business. If they can't convince you, you may be on to something.

As you implement the changes, there is a risk that some key players will not be able to make the transition to the new way of doing things. The Beatles' manager, Brian Epstein, was one such case. As the boys grew more and more disenchanted with live work, he began to fear for his livelihood. After all, he took 25 percent off the top of their gross receipts—plus expenses. Whether or not the Beatles paid their overhead, Epstein enjoyed a hefty payday after every show. It was becoming apparent that this huge source of revenue could dry up. Perhaps more important, Epstein's interests and the Beatles' were growing apart. Epstein was not at home in the studio, nor was he particularly welcome. When he sought to give input on one notable occasion, Lennon told him, in as many words, to stick to his percentages and let the Beatles worry about the music. Unable to see his way past this growing problem, Epstein began to drink heavily, abuse prescription drugs, and engage in other risky behaviors. When the Beatles finally *did* quit live work completely, he was dead within a year.

It was a very sad and premature end to an incredible success story. However, the Beatles could not have kept him alive by continuing to tour. Nor should they have tried. They would have run out of gas, and he would still have faced the same demons. Don't let the Brian Epsteins—even the ones who have helped bring you success—hold you back by clinging to old ways. It may not be easy, but there's nothing you can do that can't be done.

37
Inspiration

There will come a time when the creative juices jam. Once a business loses—quite naturally—the initial momentum that has driven it to success, it is vital that management recognize and accept the fact that forward motion may slow or even cease temporarily. And you need to be O.K. with that! It's time for a change.

As they began to accept the fact that they had retired from the road, the Beatles began to un-Beatle and went their separate ways for an unprecedented six-week holiday. Paul, ever the workhorse, relaxed by scoring a movie, *The Family Way*, with George Martin. John went to Spain to act in a movie, *How I Won the War*. George followed his soul to India. Ringo rested, and then joined John in Spain.

While apart, their core remained the band. They continued to absorb every ounce of energy in their midst to be channeled into their music. Paul's orchestral exercise would play into future recordings, George became more adept on the sitar, and John was inspired to write "Strawberry Fields Forever." This song gave the Beatles the idea to write and produce songs that could not be performed live—recordings that were, indeed, the performance. In a sense, the record toured in the band's stead.

Ideas will evaporate. Inspiration will evacuate. They must be invited to return. There is no one way to make this happen. For some, like McCartney, an industrious course of self-improvement and new work will do the trick. For others like Lennon, around this time described by one journalist as "the laziest man in England," rest and observation provide inspiration enough. When at loose ends, Lennon did little but read the newspaper, watch TV, and listen to records. But soon enough, he began to write his next clutch of masterpieces—songs inspired by watching TV ("Good Morning, Good Morning") and reading the newspaper ("A Day in the Life").

So work at getting better all the time. Or turn off your mind, relax, and float downstream. Either way, it is not dying. It may just be a creative rebirth.

38
Fans

Do you have a fan club? If not, you should. You don't have to be a star, baby, to have fans. Fans come in all shapes and sizes and with various degrees of expectation and of worship. Many CEOs and presidents are idolized by some of their employees. Many are admired in ways that would qualify as fanship.

Fans outside the office, especially in the business community, can cause problems if you do not properly acknowledge them at cocktail parties and industry gatherings. Hell hath no fury like a fan scorned. And what about fans inside the office? Although loyalty and devotion are desired traits in employees and co-workers, when these feelings go over the top, they can be one of the most disruptive influences in the workplace. These situations should be identified and dealt with accordingly and early on.

As discussed in chapter 15, the Beatles were quite skilled in the art of fan massage. Knowing that the fans held the key to their financial kingdom, they gave them what they wanted—whether it was the *shau* in Hamburg, the leather in the Cavern, or their annual Christmas messages. And of course, there was the fan club. The Beatles' fan club was to fan clubs as the Beatles were to the music world. Initially run out of NEMS, the North End Music Store, and managed by Freda Kelly, it expanded into London under the guidance of Tony Barrow. Bettina Rose was hired to serve that office and created a person named "Anne Collingham" to be the "official secretary." Fans the world over were jealous of Anne Collingham, and she did not even exist.

Place an Anne Collingham between you and your fans. Then "she" can take the heat when your fans, inevitably, are disappointed in something you do or don't do.

39
Nowhere People

Success brings with it enormous baggage—baggage that often comes in the form of humanity. Hangers-on will appear and attempt to hang from the branches of your tree. They want what you have without having to work for it, or having the talent for it. They will come from nowhere, and if you are not careful, they will try to take everything you have. They want you to know that they were with you from the start. Usually you will not remember this to be true.

Although they are benign, if not well managed, they can become malignant and grow like a cancer. If given admission and permission to hang in your tree, after establishing the most meager of *bona fides* they will soon be there night and day. They will begin to feel like they own the joint. And they have friends, many of them: nowhere people with nowhere thoughts, except for the talent of finding an occasional opportunity to make millions with just a small cash investment.

The Beatles, at least initially, had several layers of protection from the nowhere people. On the business side, Brian kept them away. Neil Aspinall and their huge Liverpool friend Mal Evans, who became their *de facto* bodyguard, seemed to swallow the Beatles whole when the nowhere people appeared in their personal orbit.

Their fame and their hectic schedule kept them isolated and they developed a unique bond: they were the only people in the history of the world to endure Beatlemania from the inside. Therefore, few had any point of reference to engage them. Sycophants quite often attempted to identify or lay claim to them. There were enough "fifth" Beatles—with claims of varying merit—to fill the Albert Hall. However, their "Mersey Mafia" still protected them from the nowhere men and women of the world.

Stay away from the nowhere people without slighting them. Some are a bit testy. Let the staff deal with them. They'll get you right where they are: nowhere.

40

Bad Influences

While the nowhere people only want to glom on to you, and get something out of you, there are others who, by contrast, want to share with you. They would love to turn you on to whatever they are doing. These are not nowhere people. They may, in fact, be somebody—relatives, friends from the past with a legitimate claim on your affections, or intoxicating new acquaintances who share the new stature you have earned. Maybe, just maybe, they have not dropped some of their bad habits. It could look like fun to join ole Flattop as he comes "groovin' up slowly." More than likely, that's a bad idea.

There is a very easy litmus test for this—if it is not legal, don't do it. You are a public figure now, or fast on your way to becoming one. Of course, everyone has seen the mug shot of a famous person or two. They are not appealing. Unless you are the rare person who can laugh off incarceration and ridicule, don't do it. Few who have been there would recommend it.

There is a famous story of the Beatles' dentist who turned them on to LSD. Though John and George stood by that story until their respective deaths, I have never seen a photograph of this dentist, nor have I read his memoirs, seen or heard any interviews, or learned of any public appearances. It is likely that once that story came to light, he felt no little discomfort, for if his name came to light, he would be subject to professional discipline and legal sanction, resulting in the loss of his livelihood. Perhaps this was John and George's revenge for what, by all accounts, was a horrendously bad "trip" for them and their wives. This dentist was a bad influence, and also lucky—LSD trips at that time sometimes resulted in accidental deaths and suicides.

There were other bad influences along the way, but none of them had a chance to take root until the touring stopped. During the whirlwind of the early years, the boys were too busy to catch much trouble. Their inner circle usually protected the group from those who might lead them astray. They were like modern-day Peter Pans—stuck in a sort of social childhood and hanging out with their Liverpool mates during the rare times when they were not together. Once the touring ended, each Beatle began expanding his respective personal sphere of influence—in positive directions for the most part. Yet the turbulence of all the drug busts of the late

1960s attests to the infiltration of disruptive negative influences as well.

The temptation offered can seem harmless and—quite frankly—like a little well-earned fun. The list of those who have succumbed only to see their careers ruined is much longer than that of those who are immune to scandal. If you're feeling invincible, light a match and hold your finger to the flame. If you're still feeling no pain, do what you want. Otherwise, behave yourself, or you will get burned.

41

Drugs

Are you having trouble sleeping yet? You know you need the rest—you have an important meeting in the morning. Finally, at four o'clock, you are only (just) sleeping. At six o'clock, when the alarm goes off, you shake your head and you're still yawning.

Now that pharmaceutical companies have made their way to mainstream television advertising, you are probably aware that prescription drugs exist to assist in every aspect of your life—whether staying awake, going to sleep, even paying attention.

The Beatles were no strangers to such drugs. In Hamburg, where they cut their musical teeth, they relied on "uppers"—very effective diet pills that contained amphetamines that were legal at the time—to help them survive their grueling sets. This was fairly common among musicians, and considered as innocuous as NoDoz is today. However, a slippery slope accompanies any chemically assisted activity. If you are taking uppers to keep going, pretty soon you are going to need the "downer" to make sure you get some sleep. If you're not careful, you may soon find that you never feel "normal" unless you are popping a pill. No problem, you say. I'm not a pill popper! But you probably do drink coffee in the morning to "get started," and maybe you even have a couple of drinks in the evening to relax or "take the edge off." There is nothing intrinsically wrong with these activities. But beware that as your stress level increases you do not rely on ever-growing quantities of these two legal but highly addictive drugs (for that is what they are).

Most of all don't let reliance on these legal drugs become a gateway to harder, illegal drugs. It has been well documented that the Beatles were turned on to marijuana by Bob Dylan during their first American tour. They, like much of their cohort, became giggling devotees, and pot would have its negative impact: Paul Mc-Cartney suffered a couple of major busts for possession years after the group disbanded and faced possible hard time in Japan. And no one can say how pot may have influenced McCartney's productivity and artistic judgment at key times in the post-Beatle era.

John Lennon did even worse, becoming addicted to heroin. He would later describe the pains of withdrawal in his solo song "Cold Turkey." Such phrases as "Temperature's rising, goose pimple bones" or "I wish I was a baby / I wish I was dead" do not paint a pleasant portrait of the experience.

Then there was LSD. After reportedly having the drug slipped into their tea by George's dentist, John and George were the first to "trip." Though the first trip was unexpected and frightening, they ultimately found LSD useful. They interpreted their sensory hallucinations, right or wrong, as insights into the slippery fabric and permeable barriers of reality. They continued to use the drug for recreational and inspirational purposes throughout the next few years. They soon persuaded Ringo to try some, and months later Paul joined his mates in the land of psychedelia. There the creativity flowed, and the songs became more inward, colorful, descriptive, and open-ended.

It would invite controversy to say that drugs had no positive impact on the Beatles' music. Quite probably without the experiences induced by LSD, some of the Beatles' finest songs would not have been written. It is equally true, however, that many of their finest songs were the result of a creative genius not engineered by any illegal substance, legal or illegal. And the drug-inspired songs themselves were written when relatively sober, as the Beatles recollected and sought to capture in song the strange and disjointed experiences brought on by their drug experiments. These sober intervals, fueled by marginally more wholesome fuels like tea, cigarettes, and fried curries, were the productive times. If the Beatles had been using all the time, these songs would *not* have been written. And they certainly never performed the master takes of their songs in the studio stoned—the results were too uneven. Ringo stated in the *Anthology* that during their times of heavy drug use, there were frequent re-recordings as stoned takes were discarded owing to their unsuitability.

The career of the Beatles is hardly a pat anti-drug lesson, but it should be noted that all of the Beatles subsequently cleaned up. Ringo went through rehab for booze and has been sober for more than twenty years. For the record, McCartney has claimed at various times to have quit marijuana. It would also be wise to note that Beatle jobs, especially after 1966, did not require them to be anywhere in particular for months at a time. Most people in business, with full-time, structured work commitments, will find their drug menu to be far from manageable. Ultimately, the Beatles found healthier ways to find their inner selves, to relax or become stimulated, and to be inspired.

So endure a sleepless night or two. Go ahead and fall asleep in that meeting. The price of the alternatives may be higher than you think.

42
Expansion

As an entrepreneur, you will usually need to spend a dollar to make a dollar. That's smart. But as your cash reserves increase, you will need to be even smarter. You will need to know when it makes sense to spend a dollar when there is no immediate cash return—and know when you're just throwing money away. These distinctions can spell success or failure for your business down the road.

You and your management team may see the need to expand operations, hire new staff, acquire more space and the fixtures, furniture, and equipment that goes along with it. Some of this additional overhead, such as customer service representatives, will yield only intangible returns, but you must be ready to invest some of your hard-earned cash in these intangibles if you wish to continue to prosper. Failing to do so will run you, your employees, and your customers ragged. You're stuck with you, but your employees and customers have a choice.

So it was with the Beatles as they developed. There were accountants and bookkeepers to keep track of what was going out and coming in. In addition, they soon needed a press secretary and a personal secretary for Brian Epstein. NEMS was growing and needed the likes of Tony Bramwell, a childhood friend of the Beatles, as a full-time operative. Neil Aspinall and Mal Evans continued on in their usual roles, and Tony Barrow was given more responsibility in managing the various offices. Barrow also expanded the fan club into London. Looking over this entire staff, not one generated revenue. They were not involved in marketing or sales or distribution. But they were necessary to the continuation and expansion of the enterprise. These are the people and resources that can turn an angry or disappointed customer—or fan—back into a lifelong devotee.

There was another layer in the Beatles' organization, the role of which was simply to keep the Beatles happy. It can be argued that the happiness of the band members was key to generating additional income. If Paul McCartney needed an ocarina, someone should find an ocarina. If John needed a lift to an art gallery, someone should deliver him and accompany him. Perhaps for this reason, many of their employees were friends of the band who eventually landed on the payroll. (It should be noted that when the Beatles realized how high their overhead had become by the late

1960s, their friends were the first to go. Of course, the accountants stayed until the bitter end.)

Few organizations will, or should, have this luxury. The performance of all organizations depends to some extent on the daily state of mind of the principals. Those who are waited on hand and foot, however, soon become petty despots. Beware of surrounding yourself with friends or minions at this stage—because of your success they will by necessity have a different posture toward you than those who started with you when you were nothing. They will spoil you and turn the office into a hangout.

So get your own coffee. Meet your friends for lunch, outside the office. Hire an accountant and some customer service representatives and give them comfy chairs. And make sure that the money you are spending is to keep your employees and customers happy, not *you*.

43

Accessibility

As the enterprise grows and the number of employees expands, there will be more and more demands on your time. The company will require more meetings, and you will become more involved in the community, perhaps serving on nonprofit boards or corporate boards. There will be social functions that a person in your position will need to attend.

Time management will become more challenging. Always remember that your accessibility to your partners and employees is of utmost importance. Suppose John or Paul had not been able to attend an early recording session, when all four Beatles played the songs pretty much live in the studio? With the occasional exception, such as "Yesterday" (a song that featured only Paul backed by a string quartet), all of them showed up or things would have ground to a halt.

One fortunate by-product of their "retirement" was that it actually spawned greater interest in their career. The constant question became, "Are the Beatles breaking up?" It is indisputable that the Beatles did some of their finest work after they stopped touring. In retrospect, however, their career had the trajectory of a rocket—a spectacular ascent, followed by a short period of weightlessness after the thrusters cease and gravity fights with momentum for control—and then, the long, inevitable free fall. The Beatles burned bright during their free fall, maybe even brighter than during their ascent, but there was only one possible conclusion. By slowing the frenetic pace of the previous four years and a schedule that kept them in the center of the media worldwide, they entered that weightless period where they could do things that no one else on earth could do—like astronauts, they seemed to fly or float effortlessly, where others, earthbound, needed to walk or crawl.

But they were there for their public, too. When they stopped touring, the Beatles grasped the importance of remaining in the public eye—in their minds, and most important, in their ears. They were available to the media for radio, television, print interviews, as well as short-form music videos, shipped to TV stations worldwide, which prefigured the development of MTV years later. As always, they communicated with their fans by way of the ever-growing fan club.

You may be entering your "weightless" stage, in which you can, by virtue of your hard work and unique experiences, do things your friends, colleagues, and competitors can't. Just remember, like the Beatles, to remain accessible to those who need you, because you need them, too.

44

Is It Over?

There will come a time following your expansion when you may question the soundness of your judgment. Unbeknown to the media, your competitors, or the investment community, your management and staff are chin-deep in research and development that will provide products or services that will change your industry forever. Or so you hope. Yet the word on the street is, "What happened to you? Where are you? What have you been doing?"

The Beatles had this experience after the release of *Revolver* and their subsequent refusal to perform publicly. From the *Revolver* release in August 1966 through spring 1967, there was no new album, the longest hiatus since 1962. (Fans had grown accustomed to two a year.) They did release "Strawberry Fields Forever" and "Penny Lane," a double A–sided single, but the record was unlike anything that had gone before. Moreover, the appearance of the group had changed, with each member sporting facial hair in various new arrangements. This prompted many people to ask, "Who are these people? What have they done with the lovable, guitar playing moptops?" Was it all over?

As you prosper, you must also improve and evolve. Before releasing new ideas to the public, however, take steps to ensure that the quality of product or material is consistent with prior works. The use of focus groups or telephone research can provide valuable, perhaps career-saving information. The Beatles were taking a big chance. They did none of this. "Only time would tell if they were right or they were wrong."

45
Advice

So far, you've taken your ride alone. Like Lennon, you found your tree, an essentially solitary exercise. You may have populated it with people of like mind; those who could help you realize your vision. But now, you may feel alone again. It is, in fact, lonely at the top—even at the Toppermost of the Poppermost. Who can understand the experiences that brought you here? Who are your peers? Relax. You are not so alone as you think. What you need is a mentor.

What? you think. Mentors are for those just starting out. I'm well established, at the top, in fact. What do I need a mentor for? It is never too late for a mentor. Others have traveled the road you're on. You don't know what you are going to find around the bend, but they do. Not only do they have knowledge to impart to you, they *understand* you. They have felt the same fire that gave you warmth, and then later maybe burned you. They too swam with the sharks and are ready to show you the tooth marks.

The Beatles were hailed as innovators even in the early days. Their style with its "Merseybeat" led the British "invasion" and dominance of world culture in the mid-1960s. But the conquerors were not too proud to pay heed to those who had something to teach. As we have noted, Bob Dylan influenced the Beatles greatly, in particular the songs "You've Got To Hide Your Love Away" and "I'm A Loser." Dylan also influenced generally their whole approach to writing pop lyrics. And they didn't just get their information from records—as peers, the Beatles and Dylan sought each other out and had long, fruitful (and often, stoned) discussions about their mutual ideas on songwriting.

It's often just such a two-way street: it is no small coincidence that after his continued contact with the Beatles, Dylan swapped his acoustic guitar for an instrument of the electric variety. The Beatles began to inspire their mentor, even as they were inspired by him. The Beatles likewise served as mentors to those around them. The Rolling Stones and the Beatles were close friends. John and Paul, by finishing "I Wanna Be Your Man" on demand in their presence, even inspired Mick Jagger and Keith Richards, one of rock's great songwriting duos, to write their own songs.

It is always a good idea to approach other movers and shakers and ask them how they accomplished what they did. More times than not, the conversation will last longer than you anticipated and yield marvelous, useful fruits. Go find your Dylan. Get the juice you need to shake things up a little.

Don't be surprised if the other party also learns a trick or two from you. And don't be afraid to share your expertise with your own protégés—to give the Micks and Keiths around you a shot at the big time. You've written your "She Loves You"—help somebody else write their "Satisfaction." It's what makes the world go 'round.

46
Positive Attitude

There is no way that a negative person can reach his full potential. That person's self precludes any chance for optimal success. He can achieve at high levels, but not the optimal—not ever. Follow the sun if that's what makes you laugh. Find others who are laughing and feeling good in special ways. They will take you to success. If your management is souring, introduce them to the story of Pete Best. The same goes for your employees. Negative people will cause damage in the end. Remember this: The same goes for you. That's right—you.

Some people are born with a positive outlook. Others gravitate toward the negative. Negativity is a weakness and can be cured through exercise. All of the Beatles, with the possible exception of

Ringo, could be crabby, get down in the dumps, and feel like the end was near. But their saving grace throughout much of the 60s was that they made one another happy. Their own company kept them positive and on track. Where John led, they followed—happily. They used creativity as a means of retaining their "positivity." Negativity would not be tolerated.

Paradoxically, it was with a quick wit and a biting tongue that Lennon was able to maintain a positive attitude among his band, by creating an "us versus them" mentality. That, coupled with continuous affirmations, such as the "Toppermost of the Poppermost" cheer, did the trick.

Keep your group happy. Keep them focused. Find the positive wherever possible in all events and all people. Positivity is as contagious as its negative counterpart. Plant and nurture the seed of positivity.

47
Second Wind

Any athlete will tell you that the "second wind" is no myth or mere figure of speech. It is a physiological experience that occurs when the body, at the point of exhaustion, somehow unlocks a hitherto-unsuspected reserve of energy to allow a performance that should, for all intents and purposes, be impossible. The key is to keep moving forward, step-by-step or stroke-by-stroke, until that magical second wind appears.

Paul McCartney had been the last of the four to see the wisdom of the band's retirement from the road. He felt that the road kept the band polished and in musical shape. Of all the Beatles, he had the greatest appetite for the show business grind and for sheer, unremitting hard work. However, after the Philippines incident, even he saw the wisdom of quitting the road while they were ahead. For the relentlessly self-improving McCartney, this capitulation was tempered by a resolution to explore the new studio-centric Beatle workspace to the fullest, to produce the "grooviest" pop masterpiece ever. The other Beatles, at first exhausted, after six weeks were only too happy to oblige. During their "vacation," George was learning not only the instrumental music of India, but Eastern philosophy as well. The knowledge Paul had gained from the scoring of the film *The Family Way* would not lay dormant. And John's writing while filming his movie in Spain would soon amaze the world.

Back to business and in the studio—an old familiar haunt—the Beatles began going through the old familiar motions. Turns out, their brief hiatus left them refreshed and ready to scale new peaks. Suddenly the "same old same old" had some new twists to it, some new energy and technique. Suddenly, this tired, wounded, energy-depleted rock and roll band was on its way to a higher branch in their tree.

You can do the same in your business. For whatever reason, the company hits the wall. But as long as you keep your group on track, doing the things they do well, covering the fundamentals, you will make progress. The injection of creative growth and expansion will be seamless as long as the members of the company are functioning in the manners implemented and rehearsed by the management. The second wind *will* appear for them just as it does for the athlete.

48
Continuing Commitment

The tree you climbed so long ago, or so it seems, has new branches and leaves. Others within the community, starting much later and with much less risk, followed your lead and achieved great success by simply doing what you are doing. They have benefited from your creativity, mistakes, lumps, bumps, and bruises. To maintain your edge, recommit to the engine at the core of your business. The idea that you conceived, nurtured, and developed to get you here may need to be nurtured still.

For the Beatles, that engine was the song. Oddly enough, the Beatles, in the midst of Beatlemania, had formulated an exit strategy of sorts. They had seen acts come and go and were very realistic about the chances of ongoing popularity. They felt the song was the key to long-term income and they were constantly in search of different angles and fresher wordplay, as well as appealing forms of musical abstraction and diversion, to make sure that when it came to a song, nobody had a leg up on John Lennon or Paul McCartney.

While touring, they wrote. When they were making movies, they wrote. They wrote in the studio, on holiday, in the bathtub, in the bed. They wrote in their dreams. Every thought and experience, everything they saw, read, or heard was absorbed and considered suitable material for a song.

Thus, when the British Invasion came full force, it was not disconcerting to the Beatles to have so much competition. For a while, it seemed that every British act that chose to grow their hair long, hang a few guitars over their shoulders, and stand around the drummer could obtain a record deal, have a number-one record, and tour the United States. There were the Kinks, the Zombies, the Who, the Rolling Stones, Chad and Jeremy, Peter and Gordon, Gerry and the Pacemakers, Billy J. Kramer and the Dakotas, Freddie and the Dreamers, Herman's Hermits, the Dave Clark Five, Manfred Mann (including their old pal Klaus Voormann), Eric Burdon and the Animals, and a host of others.

Many of these acts were managed by Brian Epstein. Peter and Gordon and Billy J. Kramer—and even the Stones on one occasion—relied on Lennon-McCartney songs for their hits. The Beatles were enthusiastic supporters of their colleagues, because of their shrewd focus on the songs as the engine of revenue. They saw the success of the other British bands as a source of income.

A rising tide lifts all boats, as they say. As the competition in your business becomes fierce, refocus on the essentials. Renew your song. Refresh it if necessary. Experiment and see if it leads you in other directions. But never abandon it. Then, just wait for the tide.

49
Delegate, Delegate, Delegate

There will come a time when it is necessary to delegate responsibility to others. It is one of the more difficult tasks that entrepreneurs face: they are carving out a piece of their soul and handing it to another person. And they seldom do it well. In most cases, the delegator micromanages the delegatee to a point of extreme frustration, at which point the delegator has spent more time than he would have if he had done it himself—and the delegatee is ready to quit. You need to get this right. You can't do everything yourself.

As the Beatles evolved they began to experiment—with drugs, with countless instruments, and with studio techniques. At times, John or Paul would have an idea for a sound—something they could hear only in their heads. They would describe the sound to George Martin or the engineer, Geoff Emerick, and tell them to find a way to produce that sound—not necessarily mechanically—in the air of the studio. Sometimes these sounds could only be achieved through the manipulation of electronic signals.

Both John and Paul came to trust the abilities of Martin and Emerick to manufacture a means of creating sounds that in many cases had never been heard before. Lennon, in particular, would often finish his performances and then retire from the studio with vague instructions, such as "put ketchup on it." One of the studio's main technical innovations of the era, automatic double-tracking or ADT, arose from Lennon's aversion to singing the same vocal over and over. Using ADT technology, Emerick could create a second vocal track by "doubling" the existing vocal track. He would then mix the two together slightly out of sync to thicken the sound—a process analogous to placing two identical photographic negatives over each other, then moving one slightly out of position to create a slightly blurred effect.

Without Emerick or Martin's assistance, these sounds would have remained trapped in John's imagination or Paul's—perhaps forever. It is not likely that they would have learned all the technical aspects of recording so that they could do it themselves, nor would it have been a good use of Beatle time. By delegating to those they had hired and then allowing them to perform their jobs, John and Paul were able to continue on with performing the song, and—equally important—with writing the next one.

Hire, train, and motivate people who share your vision and have complementary skills. Find your Emerick or Martin. Trust them and let them do their work. They won't let you down.

50
The Masterpiece

At some point, it is time to take the sum total of all your experiences and create your masterpiece. This is usually not a conscious decision—you are just doing what comes naturally to you, perhaps after a brief period of retrenchment or inactivity. The competition may think that you have given up, that you're tired, that you're done. The fact is that you have been building to this for your entire life.

With the Beatles, it was the album *Sgt. Peppers Lonely Hearts Club Band.* Arguably the most important work ever recorded and hailed by numerous publications as the best album in the history of rock and roll, *Sgt. Pepper,* as it would be forever known, defied all conventions and changed everything.

The Beatles had taken one marathon 13-hour session to create their first record. They spent four months creating *Sgt. Pepper*. Almost none of the tracks were created "live" in the studio. Instead, the bones of each track would be laid on tape. Then came a collage of individual performances, assembled painstakingly into coherence for maximum effect, then overlaid as necessary with sound effects. Sometimes the songs were built around a "rhythm" track of drums and piano. Sometimes the drums were the last thing to be added. There was no set method—the Beatles took their time making sure that each track received a unique and fresh approach. With the luxury of time, the Beatles explored every blind alley, often scrapping days of work and rebuilding the track from its basic form when a superior idea presented itself.

Widely credited as the first concept album in rock and roll, *Sgt. Pepper* purported to be a sort of variety show hosted by the fictional Sergeant Pepper and his band. In fact, most of the tracks had no relation to this theme, but framed as they were by elements of this narrative (the title track and its reprise toward the end of the album, as well as the faux biz introduction of Billy Shears [Ringo]), a certain unity of tone persisted. That tone was something wondrous—a shifting panoply of sound and sentiment that moved deftly from sleeping to waking, from wonder to joy to sorrow and back again in an instant. It was the sound of childhood, of Dorothy stepping into a Technicolor Oz, of Alice falling into Wonderland. As the final, crashing chord of Lennon's masterpiece, "A Day in the Life," resolved over the better part of a minute, the Beatles stood revealed as the untouchable masters of their art. (Several successful fellow pop musicians had been allowed to attend an orchestral recording session for this song. Some left after the session in a panic, with one purportedly considering immediate retirement the only honorable option.)

When they recorded the album, the Beatles along with George Martin, Geoff Emerick, and Brian Epstein knew that they had created something completely unique to their industry. There was some trepidation as to how it would be accepted by a wider audience. It did not take long for them to be reassured, at least by the approval of their fellow artists. After its Friday release, Jimi Hendrix appeared two days later at the Saville Theatre in London. His opening number? The title track of *Sgt. Peppers Lonely Hearts Club Band.*

It wasn't just Hendrix. To some observers, it seemed that the whole world surrendered to the Beatles that summer, with the record blasting out of every hi-fi and portable radio and open window. Never before had the world's youth, and music cognoscenti of all stripes, been so united in their admiration of one work. Nor are they likely to be so again.

Spend the time and expend the resources necessary to create your masterpiece. Don't be afraid to break the rules. Don't be afraid to take your time. Don't pay attention to the critics or the naysayers. You know what you're doing, and if you think you're on to something, go for it. You may have the next *Sgt. Pepper* on your hands.

51
Meeting Your Heroes

Heroes. Everyone has them. From a very early age, we start to take pleasure in the idea of superheroes with strange powers, replacing these later in the theater of our mind with very real figures from the world of sports, entertainment, business, or politics. Heroes provide us with vicarious relief from the mundane aspects of life, but they also provide us with role models for setting goals and tackling challenges. That may be why you bought this book: on some level, the Beatles are heroes to you.

Now that you are at the pinnacle of your career, you may get the chance to meet some of your heroes. It may be difficult to know how to act around them. In fact, some say you should never meet your heroes—the underlying thought being that they can never live up to the idealized portraits of them we carry around inside our hearts and minds. But the Beatles' interaction with their heroes—yes, they had heroes, too—shows that the truth is perhaps more complex.

Take, for example, the Crickets. Three humble gentlemen—Jerry Allison, Joe B. Mauldin, and Sonny Curtis—from Lubbock, Texas. Household names? Hardly. But together with their front man Charles Hardin Holley they created the template for the self-sufficient guitar band that wrote, arranged, and performed its own material. Sound familiar? Inducting the Crickets into the Musicians Hall of Fame in Nashville in 2008, Keith Richards said, "Without the Crickets, there would have been no Beatles—and no Rolling Stones." It is frequently noted that the Beatles even took the inspiration for their insect name from the Crickets.

Sir Paul McCartney in recent years has wasted few opportunities to honor the Crickets, even performing with them occasionally in tribute to the late Charles Hardin Holley—better known to the world, of course, as Buddy Holly. Unfortunately, the Beatles never met Holly himself (although their good friend Tony Bramwell did manage to get backstage and meet him during Holly's English tour).

Another hero—one they did meet in 1965—was Elvis Presley. The Beatles had always been huge fans of Elvis. When they finally had an opportunity to meet him, the meeting was initially awkward as the four Beatles sat and gawked at their idol. Gradually however, the men bonded over music, with Paul giving Elvis some pointers on electric bass. Further recollections of the evening among Elvis' inner circle, as well as those with the Beatles, tend to be vague and to differ—due to the intervening years and perhaps the liberal amount of marijuana the Fab Four are said to have smoked prior to the meeting.

When you meet the heroes of your industry, some will disappoint you. Others will inspire you even more in person. A few may even become your friends—though the gap between idol and worshiper is a hard one for friendship to bridge. Elvis already had his friends—the so-called Memphis Mafia—just as the Beatles already had their small circle of trusted insiders such as Mal Evans, Neil Aspinall, and Tony Bramwell. To their disappointment, Elvis politely deflected the Fab Four's invitations to join them the following evening at the house where they were staying. But it was the right thing to do. Elvis could never be the fifth Beatle, even for a night.

Perhaps the key when meeting your heroes is to keep your expectations realistic. Above all, don't overlook the fact that by now, you are probably a hero to some people. These people will seek you out. You will be tasked with responding courteously to attentions that you may not always want. Demand the respect that you have earned—but remember that you have a duty to serve, and to serve courteously and politely at all times. Treat these seekers the way you wanted to be treated at that stage. You will most certainly deal with your share of chumps and fools, but you will also meet—and help to groom—the next generation of heroes.

52

The Frustrated Partner Syndrome

If you are in the *Pepper* phase of your career, you may be riding high. Perhaps even more than usual, you are prone to—in the words of the old song—"ac-centuate the positive and e-liminate the negative." Normally, this is a helpful trait, one that is crucial to success. However, there is a potential downside. Not everyone who contributed to your success may be feeling the love. There could be a valuable partner—perhaps a junior partner—voicing legitimate, heartfelt frustration with his lot. In your cloud of self-regard and legitimate pride in and satisfaction with your achievements, you may think such a person is just having a bad day and that he will get over it. Such self-serving inferences and belittling of the problem can be costly in the long run.

During the making of what is arguably the Beatles' greatest work, *Sgt. Peppers Lonely Hearts Club Band,* John Lennon, Paul McCartney, George Martin, and Geoff Emerick (both of whom now enjoyed a creative partnership at some level with the two head Beatles) were consumed with the work. They created new benchmarks of creativity as they experimented with hundreds of sounds and effects using unprecedented recording techniques. They had animal noises, a whistle only audible to dogs, clocks, brass, a symphony, tape loops, backward this and half-speed that—everything that the LSD-inspired minds of Lennon and McCartney plus the ingenuity and years of training of the engineer and producer could muster.

Untold thousands have wished to be a fly on the wall for even one of those sessions. Yet on the *Anthology* DVD, Ringo remembers the Pepper sessions as when he "learned to play chess," and George Harrison described the period as "boring." Shocking, isn't it? Almost comical. Two men present at the birth of a new musical culture—living through an epochal moment, bored and playing chess.

So what went wrong? For George Harrison, the situation was complex. As he grew in sophistication as an instrumentalist and arranger, he began to feel stifled by McCartney's and George Martin's often detailed direction in the studio. Perhaps more important, it turned out that his talent for writing and performing his own material was deeper than anyone suspected. Early in his songwriting career, he had been given a quota of two songs per album. At first this allotment seemed adequate, but as his output grew, he began to feel stifled. Lennon and Mc-Cartney continued to write hit material faster than it could be recorded. A growing sense of inequity began to sour Harrison's outlook on the group.

Although his patience was tested by the marathon *Pepper* sessions, Starr had been relatively content with his contributions. But even he began to show signs of wear and tear in 1968, during the recording of *The White Album,* when McCartney took to erasing and overdubbing Starr's parts with his own drum performances. Ringo—perhaps the most even-keeled of the four—promptly took his toys and went home, briefly leaving the group.

Scratch the surface after *Pepper* and you have two very successful—but very frustrated and unhappy—Beatles. Harrison and Starr's plight goes to the heart of the entrepreneurial enterprise: your key partners and employees need to feel ownership—to feel like they are making valuable contributions—in order to thrive as part of your enterprise. Otherwise, no matter how successful you are, their work will not sustain them and they will become disenchanted and eventually leave you. And if they are unique and irreplaceable—as Harrison and Starr surely were—your days may be limited. Indeed, the record shows that, no matter how full of opportunity and promise the future must have looked during the Summer of Love in 1967, the Beatles had less than three years of creative life left when *Pepper* was released. Even Lennon—the first among equals—was starting to harbor reservations about being a Beatle.

What could Lennon and McCartney have done differently?

There were signposts along the way that all was not well. They could have paid attention. For example, the cover for the *Pepper* album includes photographs of some 73 individuals including the Beatles. When the designer, Peter Blake, requested that each Beatle submit a list of the images that he would like to have featured, according to some accounts Paul submitted about 120 names and Lennon, approximately 50. George requested 11 Indian gurus, and Ringo supposedly said he would go with whatever the others wanted.

What a rough, ready, and *accurate* gauge of each Beatle's sense of ownership in the Beatle enterprise! The refusal of George and Ringo to participate in the ground-breaking cover design should have made someone aware that these two were not content with their roles in the group.

Not sure how morale is among your folks? The universe will give you the metrics if you are attentive, just as it did with the *Pepper* cover. When someone complains or expresses a concern, listen to her. Listening and hearing are not the same thing. Ask yourself, why is she saying this? What drives her? Are her needs being met? Figure it out and then meet those needs.

In 1970, it was finally agreed that henceforward, John, Paul, and George would each have four songs per album; Ringo, two. By then, of course, it was too little, too late. There would never be another Beatle album. With his backlog of material, Harrison would go on to release a triple (!) album soon after the group's demise, fittingly titled *All Things Must Pass*.

Don't let this happen to you. In your situation, when someone complains, make sure you both hear *and* listen. You may think your company is Shangri-La. But if you have a George Harrison, give him more than his two songs per album or he will eventually leave for greener pastures.

53
Riding the Downturn

Eventually, any business will encounter a slow period or downturn. Some people cope better with this fact than others. As we have noted, Brian Epstein felt a lot of anxiety as he considered the Beatles' self-imposed downtime. Many of his traditional revenue streams—such as live work—were drying up, and his contract with the Beatles was coming up for renewal even as they seemed to need him less and less.

While his role was undeniably diminishing, he nonetheless managed to pull off two innovative management coups. Perhaps having been embarrassed and hurt by John Lennon's instructions to "stick with the percentages, we'll handle the music," he felt the need to prove his value to the Beatles, and to himself, before the contract expired.

One of Brian Epstein's persistent challenges was to keep the Beatles in the news once they stopped touring the world. So he was undoubtedly pleased when, in a remarkable accomplishment, he arranged to have the Beatles perform a song of their choice on the first-ever worldwide satellite broadcast. In Brian's view, this was one of his crowning achievements: the Beatles could tour the entire world in one evening without leaving London. As a manager, and one who appreciated smart, efficient work, he could hardly have been more delighted. His four charges did not necessarily share his enthusiasm. According to recording engineer Geoff Emerick, who was in the studio the day Brian visited to announce this glorious moment, the Beatles were unimpressed. In fact, they almost rejected the idea outright. Once they finally agreed, John muttered in a ho-hum manner, "Well, I guess I better write a song, then."

The song Lennon so hastily and nonchalantly penned for the event was "All You Need Is Love"—a song that has become an international anthem, even an unofficial theme song of sorts for the Beatles. As Beatles documentarian Seth Swirsky has said, "The first half of the Beatles' career was about the word *yeah,* the second half was about the word *love.*" (It is worth noting that the recent Cirque du Soleil Beatles tribute in Las Vegas was called, simply, *Love.*) This perception—the Beatles were all about love—stems largely, if not completely, from this one song. (The Beatles would not mention "love" in such broad terms again until "The End," the penultimate track on *Abbey Road.*) Without the efforts of Brian Epstein, the song would most likely never have been written.

The other management coup was to renegotiate a recording

contract so that they received percentages—perhaps literally heeding Lennon's sarcastic advice—rather than pennies for each record sold. This would become the standard for future recording contracts. There are many artists who have Epstein and the Beatles to thank for their subsequent good fortune.

Epstein was able to retool and perform what proved to be some of his best work, even as his original role all but evaporated. It is worth noting here that slow times have a way of bringing long-simmering issues and insecurities to a head. If Epstein hadn't felt guilty about taking such a huge percentage (Lennon's use of the word was probably not accidental) of the Beatles' earnings at the outset, he would not have been so fearful that they would dump him at the first chance. This fear caused him to act out in self-destructive ways, rather than gather his wits for whatever might come next. If he had taken a more equitable position at the outset, he would have raked in less money during the early years, but he might also have saved himself anxiety and guilt later on. He might even have saved his own life.

54
Confidentiality

Most world-beating people and organizations have a core group of what might be termed secrets—confidential routines, unique methods, even superstitions—that are key to their outstanding successes. Such organizations usually also have an *esprit de corps* that enables them to maintain secrecy around these items.

The challenge is, as always, maintenance. At first, you and your small cadre of associates will have an "us against them" mentality in which maintaining confidentiality—preserving organizational secrets—will be relatively easy. Maintaining confidentiality becomes more and more of a challenge as you become more and more successful. Inevitably, blips will appear on the public radar screen. Your friends and associates will perplex you with their behavior. Loose lips will sink a ship here and there. Things will "get back to you" through the grapevine or through third parties that should have been mentioned directly to you. Eventually, conflicts that arise internally, which should be resolved internally, will instead be played out in a relatively public forum. There may be certain things that you wish to keep secret. But, the fact is, in business, there are no secrets.

In the tight-knit, isolated world that they inhabited for years with only a select few, the Beatles were able, for the most part, to keep certain facts of life away from the public. As their popularity grew and they ceased touring and began to spend more time apart, more and more of the family secrets began to become public knowledge—often at perplexing and inopportune moments.

Untimely revelations usually spring from one of two motives: a desire to make oneself look good or unresolved conflict. A good example of the first motive was Paul's surprise admission to the press that he had used LSD. His statement had several immediate and long-term negative consequences: alienating a portion of the group's fan base, focusing the attention of the authorities on the group (eventually resulting in numerous drug busts), and causing the other Beatles to resent what they viewed as Paul's attempts to position himself as the "hippest" Beatle.

Conflict is the other big driver of public disputes. If unresolved conflict leads to frustration, often one of the principals will determine that the public should become aware of certain issues, particularly if those issues portray that person in a positive way. It is sometimes difficult to resist the temptation to feed one's case to the media, as if the court of public opinion is a proper mediator. This happened in the early 1970s, as Paul and John began to write a series of painful open letters on album sleeves and in music publications, detailing why each considered himself the aggrieved or innocent party in the Beatles' split. As if this wasn't bad enough, Lennon even began to write and release sarcastic ditties assailing McCartney's lifestyle and artistic output.

Do your best to maintain transparency and open communications within the organization. A lack of direct communication will inevitably result in your dirty laundry being aired in public. It is better to have no secrets, for the odds are good they will not be held in confidence for long.

Be prepared for the inevitable breach. The method for handling sensitive matters should be addressed in advance and incorporated into a written agreement, including agreed-upon standards of confidentiality and a process for dispute resolution. Such an agreement will provide clear standards that can prevent or minimize the damage that can be done to the organization by unwarranted discussions with the media or other outsiders.

55
Christmas and Religion

You may be a person of faith and feel called to participate in your religion. With religious diversity abounding in the business world, should your beliefs be manifested in your place of work? Conversely, you may be a nonbeliever. How do you handle the expression of others' religious beliefs in the workplace?

The question of Christmas is particularly vexing in this regard. In many parts of the world, the holiday of Christmas is, of course, sacred. Not so long ago, companies had no qualms about using the term *Christmas,* or explicit Christian imagery, during the holiday season. They also had no qualms about using such imagery to promote commerce, or about lavish Christmas parties where cocktails flowed freely and workplace protocol was relaxed.

The simple fact is that for most retail businesses, and for manufacturing businesses that depend upon retail distribution, the days beginning on Black Friday and running through December 25—the Christmas season—are the most important days of the year. While the commercialization of Christmas often draws the ire of the religious, Christian and non-Christian alike, the holiday has spawned a business cycle that cannot be ignored.

The record business is no exception. Despite their roots in the Church of England and the Irish-Catholic culture of Liverpool, the Beatles, in the early days, had an irreverent, if not explicitly irreligious, presence in the marketplace. And yet, at the promptings of their manager, a non-Christian, they used the occasion to send a message to their fan club each year and always had new product available in the retail outlets for the season. It is interesting to note that as early as 1963, in their recorded "Christmas" message to their fan club, they referred to the holiday as "Crimble" or "Krimble." They were careful not to step on any toes by explicitly making light of Christmas—instead, in a very Beatle moment, they created an absurd proxy holiday as the object of their (mostly) good-natured sarcasm.

Later on, of course, the Beatles began to react to the claims and demands of religion in less innocent or humorous ways. Although these reactions did not pertain to Christmas, they definitely pertained to the Beatle business. First came Lennon's notorious (at least in America) "more popular than Christ" remarks, followed quickly by his helpful clarification that Jesus was "O.K." George Harrison began to immerse himself in Indian spirituality and music, which many Western listeners considered to be somewhat dreary and monotonous.

In a short time, the Beatles had alienated many of their fans within the numerically predominant and foundational religion of America. At the same time, roughly 10 percent of their commercial output now had explicitly religious—or at least spiritual—elements that were foreign to the majority of the world marketplace. The latter development had dubious commercial value, no matter how edifying it may have been for Harrison. (It would be 1970 before he managed to make his religious beliefs palatable to a wide audience with the mega-hit "My Sweet Lord.")

What morals can we extract from this narrative? First, in any business, respect for the feelings and opinions of others and common courtesy are of utmost importance. A person's faith may be the foundation of the being of that person, and religious devotion to faith in one thing or another remains arguably an essential aspect of human nature. It is hard to imagine any circumstances in which it is appropriate or advisable to express a negative view of *someone else's* religion. Call this the Lennon Rule.

Then comes the Harrison Rule. Overtly religious forms of expression, done to extremes, tend to narrow your appeal in the marketplace. This strategy can be intentional, of course, and is not inherently a bad thing. For example, overtly Christian music is made for and marketed to Christians.

And this is not to say that religion has no place in business. For example, it is appropriate to express your private views of religion when you are being asked to violate a religious (or nonreligious) scruple. Anyone who would abandon his principles for profit would certainly abandon a client for profit. Religious conviction, appropriately expressed, can be a powerful—and positive—signature in the marketplace. Just don't let it become overcommercialized, at the peril of your business and your soul. (Think Jimmy Swaggart!)

Last, lighten up and enjoy yourself during the holidays. Don't be a Scrooge. Deal with the contradictions of business during the holiday season with good humor, as the Beatles did. Call this the Rule of Crimble.

56
Fun

Fun is just as essential to the success of any enterprise as hard work. If you or the other partners or employees are not having fun, key players will eventually leave. Engineer Geoff Emerick said that on his second day of work, he went to the studio to set some microphones and witnessed a phenomenon he had not seen before. What he saw that differentiated the Beatles from other acts in the EMI studios was that they were having such a good time together, enjoying doing what they were doing.

In fact, fun—and humor—are intimately linked with creativity. A humorous frame of mind releases thought from its normal strictures. No one illustrates this better than the Beatles. The Beatles had so much fun onstage (initially), in the studio, and in their songwriting that at times it is often difficult to tell when they are pulling your leg. A song like "Yellow Submarine" can read as a straight children's song, and yet "yellow submarine" was reportedly a slang term for a particular yellow pill current to the times. Certainly key lyric lines like "now they know how many holes it takes to fill the Albert Hall" in a "Day in the Life" contain the elements of an unsavory pun, as well as inviting more abstract interpretations. And Paul McCartney mystified many when he named "You Know My Name (Look Up The Number)" as his favorite Beatle song of all time. However, his choice of this patchwork quilt of humorous set pieces, which resembles nothing so much as the soundtrack to a particularly ludicrous Monty Python sketch, makes perfect sense when you understand the importance of humor and fun to the Beatles' work.

When things cease becoming fun, nothing else matters. When the Beatles quit touring in 1966, they could command the highest prices and sell out the largest stadiums. Yet they were so unhappy that they preferred to retreat to the studio than continue on the road. Money and success could not compensate for a lack of enjoyment. They were taking an enormous risk. No band had ever survived on record sales alone. But they bravely chose to retreat to where the fun and humor still lived.

Unfortunately, within about eighteen months the fun would fade from the studio as well. Emerick himself would later resign his position as the Beatles' engineer—a position coveted by almost every sound engineer in the world—due to the tension and misery he encountered in the studio. And as Ringo and George became bored or disillusioned with studio work, each would briefly leave and return to the group before its final dissolution. Such instability was a far cry from the team spirit the Beatles displayed in the early years, fueled largely by the sense of humor they shared and the fact that the work was fun.

Misery may love company, but your company cannot survive misery. Make the experience enjoyable, any way you can. This effort is key to maintaining high levels of creativity, and to retaining key personnel. When budgeting, allocate resources—real resources—for fun.

You should pay attention to whether people are enjoying their work or not, not just to whether they are doing their work well. If they are not enjoying their work, it is prudent to intervene and to determine why. If the problem can be resolved, by them or by you, resolve it! If not, it may be time for you to encourage them to find a new line of work. No one's interests are well served in the long run by a partner or employee who is not enjoying what she is doing. Eventually, attitudes will sour and the quality of work will suffer.

Think about it. Though it scarcely seems credible, John Lennon and George Harrison, and to a lesser extent Ringo—although wealthy and successful—each came to hate his job as much as any overstressed and underpaid white-collar worker could possibly hate hers. If it could happen to the Beatles, it can certainly happen to your company. Don't let it!

57
Meditation

Have you ever had a great idea in the shower? There you are, minding your own business, with your mind more or less completely blank, when out of nowhere comes the solution to a pesky, persistent problem—or perhaps a completely new creative concept. This kind of thing can also happen when you are driving the well-known route to and from work or the grocery store, or at any time the conscious mind is on autopilot, otherwise engaged, or hardly engaged at all.

Most of us enjoy this experience relatively infrequently on a "catch as catch can" basis. But wouldn't it be great if, by habit and discipline, we could experience these kinds of mini-epiphanies every day? Guess what? We can! In fact, moments in the shower or on the road are a kind of meditation, which, if practiced deliberately, can yield true benefits. Like humor, the placid, nonspecific frame of mind created by meditation is a wonderful tool for gaining access to the powers of the subconscious mind. It's almost as if such moments create a blank canvas that the subconscious mind cannot resist painting on. Meditation dates back more than 5,000 years, and can be practiced in a number of ways. Many CEOs and leaders find that thirty minutes of daily meditation can be as refreshing as a three-hour nap or an entire night of sleep. When the mind is rested, it can accomplish feats that are otherwise impossible.

The Beatles were slightly ahead of the curve in this as in other matters. In 1967, after *Pepper*, as the Beatles continued to search for new sources to spur their creativity, they eventually looked beyond mind-expanding drugs. Drugs had provided inspiration, to be sure, but the effect was temporary and the drugs were expensive, illegal, and not without unpleasant side effects. The Beatles needed to recharge their batteries, to find a new direction.

In the late summer of 1967, the Beatles attended a lecture offered by Maharishi Mahesh Yogi, who headed the Spiritual Regeneration movement, a group that Patti Harrison had joined in February. In the lecture in London, the Maharishi explained to his audience that they could meditate thirty minutes daily and reach inner peace and find spiritual energy. The Beatles realized that such spiritual energy had the potential to renew them and give birth to creative energy.

Following their lecture in London, the Beatles were invited to Bangor, Wales, for a series of lectures by the Maharishi that would span several days. They decided to attend the sessions in Wales and were so taken by the experience that they would eventually follow the Maharishi to India for weeks of instruction. During this time, the Beatles' productivity as songwriters reached its peak. In the absence of drugs and of the other distractions of London's nightlife, the Beatles completed close to forty songs that would become the backbone of what became known as *The White Album*.

By and large, the Beatles became somewhat disillusioned with the Maharishi after a few weeks. Lennon, typically, was impatient and upset that the Maharishi did not reveal the secret of life to him sooner rather than later. Only George Harrison openly continued his practice until his death and continued his loyalty to the teachings of the Maharishi—perhaps recognizing that the lesson was more important than the teacher.

Perhaps some of you are balking at these ideas because of their exotic qualities or their insubstantial nature. It's all well and good to chase the Maharishi around as a Beatle, you may be thinking, but as a businessperson, you can't touch or count the benefits of tuning out and turning on. We ask you to keep in mind two things. First, some of the Eastern concepts and practices of transcendental meditation not only have ancient roots, but also have already reconstituted themselves successfully several times in the West. A good example is the practice of cultivating a certain watchfulness or detachment from your own thoughts, in order to defuse their immediate impact on your emotions and actions. This concept has become one of the cornerstones of cognitive behavioral therapy, an empirically proven therapeutic approach to mental and emotional disorders that may be one of the twentieth century's most significant advances in that area. Even more recently, Eckhart Tolle has made a fortune repackaging some of these concepts and peddling them in his books and on *Oprah.*

Second, consider that the mind of the entrepreneur is his greatest resource. Why ignore the potential to expand the capabilities of your mind in a safe and legal way? It makes sense to at least explore the practice of thousands of years of mental and spiritual discipline. If it's not your cup of tea—granted, meditation is not for everybody—you will always have the shower.

58
Death

Although death is inevitable, it is often ignored in business dealings. There is a powerful superstition that lives within each one of us that makes us feel that by thinking or talking about death, somehow we are summoning it. Our instinct of self-preservation causes us to sweep death under the rug. But it lies in wait for all of us.

In companies and partnerships, it is crucial to have buy-sell agreements in place that clearly stipulate how the estate of a deceased partner will dispose of his interest in the company. These agreements can be funded with "key man" insurance policies held by the principals, with the company as the beneficiary. Under this scenario, the company should not have to deplete its funds to purchase back shares or pay off debts, because it can use the pay-out from the policy for this purpose. Depending on the size of the policy, it may also have some additional funds on hand to weather any transitional downturns in revenue caused by the partner's untimely death. Such policies should be initiated from the outset and updated as the business grows.

"Wait a minute," you say. "You're bumming me out! I'm young; I'm not going anywhere!" You're probably right, but there are hundreds of examples of successful entrepreneurs who have been killed during their youth. An inordinate number of them have been killed piloting their own planes, or in other reckless, thrill-seeking activities that often follow success. The driving, risk-taking personality that pushes many to success may invite opportunities to tempt fate in other areas. Even if you're not a thrill seeker or risk taker, entrepreneurs are just as likely as the general population to die of diseases such as cancer, from other natural causes, or from accidents.

A business that is prematurely robbed of its young leadership is a business in crisis. With no succession plan, the business is probably doomed. The succession plan *must* be in place. Following an event as devastating as death, there is no time for guesswork or subjectivity in attempting to determine what the decedent would have wanted, or who will fill the authority and credibility gap within the organization and with clients and customers.

Brian Epstein, the Beatles' manager, was a case in point. When he died on August 27, 1967, he was just thirty-two years of age. Thirty-two! At this tender age, he had already accomplished more than any entertainment manager of his day. His descent into the Cavern on November 9, 1961, had wound up making four scruffy youngsters from Liverpool the most famous people in the entire world. He had shepherded them from the steamy bowels of their local rock and roll club to play before royalty and millions of fans across the globe. He arranged the Beatles' partnership with George Martin, served as best man at their weddings, and hired medical personnel to treat them when they were ill. Only five years Lennon's senior, he served as the father figure for the band. From "Love Me Do" to *Sgt. Pepper,* he was there. He fed them and clothed them, and now he was gone, having taken an overdose—most agree an accidental overdose—of sleeping pills.

What happened next? In part, because there was no key man insurance or other agreement, the finances of NEMS were in disarray upon his death, and his personal assets had to be sold to satisfy debts to the company. More important, because there had been no effective succession planning, there was no one at NEMS with the credibility or authority to manage the Beatles (although there were several who would like to have tried). It is difficult to overstate the effect this management vacuum had on the group. The argument has been made that it was the lack of Epstein's direction and authority that led to the Beatles' subsequent dereliction of purpose and eventual breakup so soon after the highs of 1966 and 1967. (Lennon himself expressed that view in subsequent years.) Although they tried, the Beatles simply could not manage themselves.

It is never too early to start planning, and doing. Remember, these issues practically knee-capped the Beatles in their mid to late twenties, when they were in full flight. Fight your fears and make sure the infrastructure is in place should a key person go down— even you. That way, you will increase the odds that all the things you've built up will continue to benefit your colleagues and loved ones long after you are gone.

59
Emotions

As a leader, you must show passion in your work, day in and day out. Passion, however, is different from emotion. There are no hard and fast rules governing the display of emotion in the workplace. Often, we don't have a problem expressing positive emotion. However, negative emotion—such as anger, sadness, or disappointment—can be hard to express appropriately. As a result, many resort to hiding or "stuffing" all negative emotion. While this strategy maintains a semblance of peace and order in the short term, in the long term it will backfire and create greater turmoil.

Over most of their career, the Beatles showed little actual emotion outside their music. They appeared cheerful—even happy—

during their early barnstorming successes. Gradually, however, the smiles were replaced with poker faces or, at best, ironic smiles for the camera. Their responses to media inquisitions, for all their humor, were always somewhat aloof. They made light of their harrowing escape from the Philippines and the vitriol caused by the "bigger than Jesus" flap, even though time would prove that these had been deeply traumatic, life-changing incidents. They rarely discussed, even among themselves, their private sources of pain: Lennon's abandonment by his parents and the subsequent death of his mother (which left him feeling twice orphaned), the death of McCartney's mother, the loneliness of Ringo's sickly childhood, or Harrison's growing frustration with his "little brother" role in the band.

The Beatles were hard men, or would have had you believe that they were hard men. They seemed to carry that public detachment into their personal and private lives, at times causing great pain to those who loved them—for example Brian Epstein, who was frequently the butt of Lennon's humor. There were several possible causes for this behavior. In addition to the hard roles men have historically been called upon to play and how such roles typically affect behavior, their Liverpool upbringing influenced their demeanor. They were tough guys coming out of a tough town. Joey Molland of Badfinger, who saw the Beatles in their Cavern days and later came to know them quite well, said that they came out onstage with a swagger and wouldn't take anything off anyone. That was the Liverpool way.

Another possible explanation is the overriding ethos of "cool" that permeated 1960s culture. The workings of this philosophy can be clearly seen in the movie *Let It Be*. In this film, which unintentionally diagrammed the dissolution of the Beatles, emotions—anger, frustration, sadness, desperation—are seething just beneath the surface. Yet none of the Beatles wanted to be the first to "crack," the first to lose his cool. And so each withdraws just short of a meaningful exchange that would make progress of any kind possible. The gung-ho McCartney tries the hardest, but even he is unable to show how much the behavior of the other Beatles is hurting him. Perhaps he felt, not without reason, that to do so would have made him seem weak. It is hard to imagine Lennon, whose own emotional life was in tatters, responding charitably to an open display of emotion from McCartney. And that points up the second great pitfall of emotion in the workplace or any public forum: the perception—whether fair or not—that an overt display of emotion is a sign of weakness.

There are some simple tools that can help working groups—or anybody—over these hurdles. It may have been that for lack of these tools, the Beatles were lost. The key tool is to be able to talk about your own negative feelings—even those caused by others—honestly yet dispassionately. When your negative feelings are caused by the behavior of others, first clearly describe to them the specific behavior and then how it makes you feel. The other party may not recognize the effect his actions are having on you. Alternatively, if his behavior is purposeful, your clear description of its effect may shame him into making changes. At the very least, it can jolt him out of passive-aggressive mode and force him to deal honestly with his own motives and emotions. The more practice with this tool you get, the easier it will be to avoid becoming overtly emotional yourself. Start now!

60
Laying an Egg

In earlier chapters, we have talked about the early and inevitable mistakes we make and the failures we experience, and how to deal with them. These mistakes are born of inexperience and over-enthusiasm and are usually easily forgiven by the marketplace. After all, all of us make mistakes on the way up.

However, there is another, later, and more pernicious kind of mistake—the one that tends to occur when you're at the top. When you are flying high, the marketplace seems to take a certain perverse pleasure in your missteps, and will judge you more harshly. When you're on top, the pressure to stay one step ahead, up until this point a positive force, can often drive you to go a bridge too far. Perhaps you're tired or distracted. Perhaps you have simply developed a little too much confidence in your own judgment. The marketplace doesn't care—when you stumble, it will come down hard on you.

Up until 1967, there were a lot of things that *could* have—should have—scuttled the Beatles' career, but didn't. They had built their initial success using unique, complex chords and arrangements, strange haircuts, an unorthodox stage presence, and a dry, sarcastic sense of humor. Yet they still charmed the socks off the world. They survived horrible record and merchandising deals—only corrected in 1967—that gave them pennies where they should have earned pounds. Yet they still managed to pile up about two million pounds in capital reserves. As time wore on, they had snubbed royalty, belittled Jesus Christ, and admitted to taking illegal drugs. They had been full participants in the burgeoning sexual revolution, taking advantage of all the sexual perks of being the world's biggest pop stars. If this had been better publicized, their behavior might well have earned them widespread censure. Yet none of it stuck.

Finally, out of sheer cussedness, they had declined to tour to promote a record album—almost offhandedly inventing a new business model and changing the record industry forever with the elaborate *Sgt. Pepper.* In short, by 1967 the Beatles seemed just about infallible.

Then came the *Magical Mystery Tour.* Based on the idea of a mystery tour, a uniquely English tradition in which tourists gather to take a bus to an undisclosed holiday location, the movie had little or no structure. The music, though fine, was not fresh and surprising the way *Pepper* had been. *Magical Mystery Tour* was Paul McCartney's attempt to refocus the Beatles, but his efforts collided with John Lennon's uncontrollable imagination and there was no Brian Epstein to exert his major strength—to protect his boys from themselves.

The critics universally viewed *Magical Mystery Tour* as an overindulgent, make-weight trifle. The Beatles had stepped well outside their field of expertise. Although they continually broke musical barriers with their music, they were not filmmakers—not writers, not producers, not directors. Perhaps after the making of *A Hard Day's Night* and *Help!*—in which they played themselves— they had come to believe that by simply being themselves, they could dispense with the niceties of a script. They were very much mistaken.

Still, why should this relatively innocuous movie be regarded as such a great *failure?* The answer is simple: the higher you fly, the farther you have to fall. If any other band, even the Stones, had put it out, it would still have been viewed as a half-baked curio but not as a *failure.*

Learn this lesson. As you coast at the top, resist the urge to do something for the sake of doing something. Vet your judgment against that of your trusted advisers. Don't become overconfident. You couldn't do it all at the beginning, and you certainly can't do it all now. In the absence of Brian Epstein, who had been dead only a few months, there was a leadership vacuum and a lack of purpose in the Beatles' camp that made *Magical Mystery Tour* possible. (It is interesting to consider whether Epstein would have approved of such a project.)

If you lose one or more of your key advisers, as the Beatles did, go slow for a while. If you miss an opportunity or two, so be it. Others will come along. It is more important at this point for you to maintain the credibility in the marketplace you have worked so hard to establish. This is not to say that your primary motivation should be to fear mistakes, but rather to say that your mistakes at this stage will be both easier to avoid with due diligence, *and* more costly without it.

61
If You've Got Trouble

At some point, every enterprise experiences a period of prolonged troubles. Maybe the organization starts leaking money as the result of a strategic mistake, or picks the wrong management at a crucial juncture. Maybe—and this is a long shot—one of the principals abruptly leaves his young family and then publishes frontally nude photographs of himself and his eccentric new lover.

If you're like the Beatles, who didn't do things by halves, it could be all three (and it gets rather juicy from here on out). Although they would still make some great music—in fact, some of their greatest music was still to come—sadly, for the Beatles, the "salad days" were over. Nothing would ever be as easy as it had been before, and their path would be full of stumbling blocks—many of them self-created.

The chaotic aftermath of Epstein's death continued to take its toll on the Beatles' fortunes. Portentously, the *Magical Mystery Tour* film was the inaugural release of something called Apple Films. In late 1967 and early 1968, Apple Records, Apple Retail, Apple Music, and assorted short-lived undertakings based on fleeting Beatle whims, came into being under the loose rubric of a corporate entity called Apple Corps Ltd. Almost all of these enterprises lost money continuously and extravagantly. There are many stories of the whys and hows of Apple. It began out of the most time-honored reason for going into the entertainment industry: as a strategic business loss for tax purposes. Thus, while Apple can be seen retroactively as a mistake, in fact it was a roaring success in true Beatle style if one keeps in mind that it was *designed* to lose money. That it did, in amounts far beyond the wildest imaginings of its creators. By the end, Apple had devoured its initial capital and then some. The Beatles had each overdrawn their personal corporate accounts. Perhaps worst of all, they *still* faced crushing personal tax liabilities.

The Apple debacle is instructive in numerous ways. A reorganized Apple eventually became very profitable by focusing on its one reliable franchise—the music of the Beatles. By that time, however, the Beatles themselves were history, partly as a result of the financial stresses caused by Apple Corps Ltd. If the Beatles had had Epstein—or some other reliable and even moderately competent businessperson—in their camp at this crucial juncture, they might well have bypassed some of the pain on the way to the eventual gain. They could have controlled their corporate losses in accordance with a strategic plan, curbed their personal tax liabilities, and created a music company through which they would have enjoyed ever-increasing amounts of control over their own artistic and commercial destiny. Instead, they diversified into businesses they knew nothing about (more on this in the next chapter), lost much more money than they intended, and did nothing to improve their tax situation.

When you hit troubled times, don't let them sweep away all the gains you have made. Be cautious about entering new markets, and don't get too clever with your tax strategy! You cannot completely avoid trouble, but you can minimize self-inflicted injuries. Get professional, objective, third-party help in all of these cases to make sure you don't lose the farm.

62
Stay Focused on Your Strengths

The Beatles were not alone in their mistakes. The list of self-made millionaires who lost it all on their second venture is a long one. Athletes and singers opening restaurants, actors making films, writers opening publishing companies—the outcome is often failure. The reason? As a company grows and profits, and success is added to success, the gut feeling grows that the model for the success in one industry will carry over into another field with little effort. The temptations are particularly strong when the two industries appear to be similar or somehow related.

Apple Corps Ltd. illustrated this principle in spades. Apple's open-handed business policies began out of a need to disburse surplus money before the taxman got hold of it, and the Beatles' choices about what industries to enter were not accidental or haphazard. The Beatles' stock in trade was the making and commercial exploitation of music. Why not diversify into the electronic equipment used to make their music? Why not sell the groovy style of clothing they wore while they were making it?

What the Beatles forgot was that they entered into their original business to become the best in the world. With talent, sweat, and years of work, they *had* become the best. In their business. But being the best is only half the challenge—maybe not even half. The other half of the trick is to stay the best at the core business, and this is where even world-beating organizations like the Beatles can falter. Starting new ventures can cause you to lose your focus. And creating a whole new way of doing business—as the Beatles intended—is even more risky.

Instead of creating new companies from whole cloth, the Beatles might have fared better had they bought existing companies in the desired fields and entered into joint ventures, strategic alliances, or other partnerships. The Beatles' foray into the field of studio electronics is instructive here. In the late 1960s there were several talented recording engineers and technical staffers—Dick Swettenham at Olympic and Malcolm Toft at Trident, for starters—bursting with ideas for new and improved studio equipment. Swettenham and Toft would go on to start successful companies manufacturing studio consoles well into the 1970s. (In fact, the Beatles' short-lived Apple Studio would purchase one of the first consoles from Helios, the company that Swettenham started with Glyn Johns and Richard Branson.)

Lacking the business sense of Richard Branson, and with no advice from business experts—the Beatles didn't partner with a Swettenham or Toft. Instead, they put their money behind Alex "Magic Alex" Mardas, a charming dabbler whose primary qualification for the job seemed to be that he amused John. Lacking any kind of stake in the business or incentives to produce, he simply lounged on their payroll, for years. What results he did produce were unusable.

In later years, McCartney began to diversify his holdings by investing his hard-earned lucre in other successful, established music publishing companies (such as the catalog of Buddy Holly), effectively bypassing the treacherous waters of the startup process of a new venture. Paul demonstrated that he had absorbed at least some of the hard-won lessons of Apple.

63
Losing Sight of the Goal

Years—or perhaps months—into a venture, you may have the opportunity to expand, grow, experiment with new products, or completely overhaul the operation. Any or all of those ideas could work, and may even be in order, but you must not lose sight of the initial goal.

In early 1968, the Beatles retreated to Rishikesh, a small village on the Ganges in India to continue their studies with the Maharishi. George and John spent nearly two months there before realizing that the Maharishi was only human, and they saw the limitations associated with that humanity. (They alleged he began making advances on Mia Farrow, one of their fellow travelers at the retreat.) Whatever the truth of the matter, as John Lennon told Larry Kane, "We came back rested to become businessmen."

Wait a minute. Did the Beatles go off to Hamburg to become yogis-in-waiting or to open a retail clothing boutique, a record label, or a film company? Absolutely not. Originally, their goal had been simply to be the Toppermost of the Poppermost. They could have saved themselves a lot of pain in 1968 by rededicating themselves to that goal. Instead, they got caught up in the grandiosity of the times that were very self-consciously a-changing, some forever not for better.

Their first order of business as businessmen was to announce the Apple Foundation of the Arts, offering grants to songwriters, moviemakers, and recording artists. They even came to the United States to announce the company's opening. Their "Western Communism" would allow talent to record an album or make a film at no expense. They spent the next six months promoting Apple records and various other Apple enterprises. Remember that they had been in India for an extended stay and had spent the six months prior to that on *Magical Mystery Tour,* for a grand total of roughly sixteen months. By contrast, during the sixteen-month period from February 1964 through June 1965, they had completed two world tours; starred in two successful films (conceived, scripted, and directed by professionals); written, recorded, and released five albums; and made hundreds of television appearances. It seems that when they decided to become businessmen, their business lost its greatest asset.

Perhaps your group, too, has lost sight of the initial goal. Like the Beatles, chances are that the original goals are still the best plan. Double back and check yourself against the original goals. If the goal was monetary, be sure to track your success. Was your goal to build a company and sell it? Where in the process are you now? If your goal was to achieve greatness in an area or industry, has it happened? Or have you gradually and without noticing begun to drift into other areas?

Of course, you may no longer find your initial goals fulfilling or meaningful, but that does not mean that your current enterprise is the correct venue for exploring your new dreams or curiosities. Take a sabbatical. Pick up a new hobby. But don't damage the business you have worked so hard to create by bending it to purposes that it wasn't designed to fulfill.

64

It Doesn't Get Any Easier

As businesses grow and flourish, the founders may begin to feel that they should be rewarded for their institutional knowledge. Perhaps they have been recognized in their community for their successes—sought out by wannabes, the media, and peers for insight and knowledge. Maybe they feel they should be able to profit from their success.

It is a maxim of "get rich quick" or "pyramid" schemes that at first a person must do all the work for little or no money. Then as he advances, he performs only some of the work for more of the money. Until finally, at the top, he performs none of the work for most of the money. Indeed, there is some element of truth to this theory in partnerships such as law firms, where golf-loving senior partners and even elderly founding partners who no longer practice but "keep an office" skim huge percentages off the work of junior underlings. But in most businesses, it's pay to play, do or die, until the end.

While the Beatles may not have subscribed to the "pyramid" idea explicitly, it seems that they expected that having a business associated with their name would guarantee its success. That seems to have been the philosophy of Apple Corps, at least in part. But that "something for nothing" ideal failed within months: the Apple boutique went out of business in July of 1968, liquidating its inventory by simply giving it away to the public. The film division likewise was going nowhere.

Apple Records was the exception. The label scored a huge success with its first release, a single recorded by a group of London businessmen who still called themselves the Beatles. The song was titled "Hey Jude," and the businessmen, having recognized the value of this band and the opportunities offered by media such as television, performed the song on *The David Frost Show* in their first televised performance in two years. And now it wasn't just any record label suggesting they appear on the telly—it was *their* record label. Perhaps for the first time in a year, the ghost of Brian Epstein was resting easily.

A sort of prophecy from their first American press conference surprisingly came true. Back then, they were asked how they had achieved their success, and Lennon quipped, "If we knew that we'd form another group and become managers." In 1968, they showed a real gift for picking talent. They discovered Mary Hopkin, who had a big hit on Apple Records with a recording of "Those Were the Days," and another hit with a McCartney song, "Good Bye." They also signed a young James Taylor, who never had a hit on their watch, but who later proved that their instincts were right. Another band, the Iveys, evolved into Badfinger and recorded numerous hits for the label.

The Beatles accomplished their success as performers with a strict work ethic, and ascended to the top of the world during a rigorous three-year schedule. They learned in the first six months of Apple Records that to achieve success in another realm, the work ethic by trained, talented individuals must continue. Simply coasting on a famous name did not work. Fortunately, during their journey to India, they had continued to write. All of the Beatles had songs in one or another stage of completion, by some estimates roughly forty in all. They recorded one of their most successful albums in 1968. Its success defied marketing principles when, untitled and packaged in stark white, it became a best-selling album. Officially called simply *The Beatles,* the album was, and is, referred to as *The White Album.*

When they returned to the studio to record the songs, the production staff realized that the Beatles were not having fun anymore, and did not get along. John, Paul, and George took to working alone in the studio, calling the others in only when necessary. Not only that, they were insulting and abusive to those around them to the point that Geoff Emerick quit his position as engineer.

It cannot be overstated: beware of dalliances in other industries, of spreading your team's store of goodwill too thin. Nothing is free; every effort comes with a price. Make sure you focus your efforts—and those of your team—where they count.

65
Mutual Respect and Appreciation

Your partners were your friends when you started. You have become closer through all the challenges, obstacles, and victories. However, there is a risk with such closeness. Familiarity can begin to breed contempt, or perhaps a certain neglect or perceived abandonment within the relationship.

Each of the members brings something special and unique to the group. At first, the contributions were celebrated. "Wow, I can't believe you came up with that! Brilliant!" Those congratulatory remarks continue through the "honeymoon" phase. As the business evolves, these extraordinary accomplishments become ordinary to the other members, even expected or required. Watch out for this! It is a slow and insidious killer of your *esprit de corps*.

During the recording of *The White Album,* the conditions in the studio deteriorated to the point that even the ever-amiable Ringo could take it no longer, and he left. He later sent word that he was leaving the group. He felt they no longer needed him. (He often remarked that he was the drummer in a band that consisted of three frustrated drummers, plus him.) When the others learned that he had left, each went to talk to him individually to let him know that the group depended on him and that he was, in their view, the best rock drummer in the world. When he told John of his feelings, John said that he felt it was *him* that the others wanted to leave. George also felt the others wanted him out, while Paul thought he was driving everyone mad, and that they wanted *him* out.

Clearly some sort of vital communications breakdown had occurred. When Ringo returned to the studio, his drum kit was covered in flowers, compliments of the other band members. It would have had a greater effect if they had done it before he left, of course. And what about John? Or Paul? How often did they tell each other how great they were? Did they ever?

Geniuses need positive reinforcement. As members of your business continue to perform well, compliment them as if it were their first time to attain excellence. Consistently stellar performances are rare. When someone regularly excels, shout it from the rooftops.

66

Spouses and Significant Others

Even workaholics need companionship. It is not a weakness, and behind many successful people are companions without whose support the person would not have succeeded, at least to the extent he did. The role of these "significant others" in the composition of the company can be positive for the organization, when managed properly. Or they can be negative. John Lennon and each of his two wives made waves for the Beatles. The first wave was manageable. The second wave was a tsunami.

When John married his first wife, Cynthia, she was pregnant with their son Julian. Since marrying one's pregnant girlfriend was the proper thing to do and John loved Cynthia, why not? Brian Epstein, fearing it would hurt the popularity of the band among their largest market segment, single females, thought it would be better to keep the marriage a secret. However, that did not work for long. When the Beatles appeared on *The Ed Sullivan Show,* a graphic of the name of each Beatle was displayed under their respective images. Under John's name, the line added said, "Sorry girls, he's married!" It was reported that this did not set well with John and Brian, but it was the only thing that didn't that night and all ill will was swept under the carpet.

All of the Beatles had girlfriends during Beatledom. Eventually, Ringo married Maureen Cox, George wed Pattie Boyd, and Paul was engaged to actress Jane Asher. These marriages and engagements had no measurable impact on the popularity of the band.

Enter Yoko Ono. The story of John and Yoko is long and controversial. There are as many tales as there are tellers, depending, to quote former Epstein protégé Andrew Loog Oldham, upon "point of view and paymaster." She certainly arrived with a bang, accompanying John into the sacred ground of EMI studios during the recording of *The White Album.* She took a seat beside John and never left. She even walked with him when he went to the bathroom. The Beatles, even though they were growing apart at the time, remained a tight-knit group and seldom let outsiders into the inner circle, much less the inner sanctum of the studio.

Yoko's presence was a distraction to the other Beatles as well as to George Martin. Many have concluded that Yoko broke up the Beatles, but that is too simple and simply not true. John's anti-social and passive-aggressive maneuver of introducing a stranger to the Beatles' sessions without preamble or explanation, no matter how much he loved her, demonstrates how lack of mutual regard can create toxic situations very quickly.

Though the fault was John's, Yoko could never remain a passive observer for long. Indeed, it would not have been fair to expect her to remain so, given the obviously privileged position she had been thrust into by John. Eventually, she found her way onto certain tracks, such as "The Continuing Story of Bungalow Bill." It is unclear whether the other Beatles welcomed her input. Perhaps more important, and corrosively, John and Yoko formed a private enclave within the Beatles' inner sanctum. Although there is no record of it, it would be highly unusual if one or two of Yoko's opinions about this or that groove or song weren't floated, if only by John, as a way of pleasing and appeasing his new lover.

This is where it can get tricky. In many situations, a member of the organization may continually refer to suggestions a spouse has made about how to better run the operation or how to deal with a particular situation. Usually this is only tolerated by others, rather than welcomed. If the others had wanted to include the spouse, they would have arranged to hire the person. If you are in the habit of referring to the suggestions made by your significant other, tread lightly. It is difficult for someone outside the company to offer objective input. After all, they have only the information provided them by their husband or wife. Beware of repeating references, such as "Bill feels that we are way off base here" or "Bill thinks we should hire three new people so that we can take some time off" or "Bill thinks we should get a raise."

Bill, like Yoko, is a four-letter word. If this is you, stop it now. If it is someone else, take her aside and show her that picture of Yoko sitting under the piano. She'll get the message!

67
Company Retreats

At some point, somebody may have the bright idea to reward the team by taking them off-site on a conference or retreat. The reasoning is that at the retreat, they can bond in a more casual, social setting. After they let their hair down, perhaps they can work through some entertaining exercises that teach teamwork, goal setting, or problem solving and conflict resolution. The company may hire guest speakers to expound certain philosophies and—among other things—instruct people how to "think outside the box." Then they can unwind with a drink or two—or ten. When they return to the office, the reasoning goes, their work will be enhanced by the improved personal connections they feel. This may well be the case, but beware! When the normal workplace rules are relaxed, chaos can—and often does—ensue. Corporate retreats, at best, are mixed blessings.

The Beatles' second retreat—with the Maharishi in Rishikesh—resulted in a burst of songwriting productivity, but also in their disastrous decision to become "businessmen." Their first off-site retreat was Hamburg. What occurred there is exemplary of what can happen at these off-site gatherings.

On the positive side, the band improved and bonded. But then came the personal tumult. Paul became exasperated with Stuart (John's friend) and persuaded John to fire Stuart. Klaus Voormann had befriended the Beatles and introduced them to his girlfriend, Astrid Kirchherr—then Stuart began to have sex with Klaus's girlfriend. The Beatles grew apart from Pete Best—more backstabbing—and began their courtship dance with Ringo Starr. To add fire to the already volatile personal dynamics, they stayed drunk most of the time, became dependent on pills, and had sex with multiple partners, many of them strippers.

Strippers. Betrayal. Alcohol-and-pill-fueled mayhem. Yes, this could be your retreat if you are not careful. (Some of you may be rubbing your hands in anticipation.) Beware! Although runaway mischief and misrule is unlikely, any behavior resembling it is even more destructive among working (and especially married) adults, with their real-world responsibilities, than it is among teenaged rock and rollers.

Off-site overnight retreats have led to the demise of many small companies. Don't let yours be one of them.

68

When Leaders Lose
It—Adolescent Behavior

When you are successful, there are a thousand things that can take you down. One of them is adolescent behavior on your part or by another key player in your organization. In a way, business lives mirror private lives. For example, learning the basic skills of a business is similar to learning to walk. Each industry has its own language; ergo, to communicate, one must learn to speak that language. And rising through the ranks to the top is akin to the physical body reaching maturity, with its enhanced capabilities and appetite for challenge and excitement. During your "business adolescence," you will make mistakes and find yourself in awkward situations as the demands on you exceed your experience or capabilities. Though painful, these experiences are crucial to your business development, just as adolescence is to your growth into adulthood.

All of this is normal. It becomes inappropriate only when you mix your personal experiences as an adolescent—or retrograde adolescent behavior—with your business activities. The temptation can be strong, particularly for leaders, who are less answerable than subordinates to accountability structures. As a result, when a leader misbehaves, the marketplace may impose its own—much tougher—sanctions.

In a way, the Beatles were forced into an early and superficial personal maturity in order to survive Hamburg and the grueling climb to fame. Consequently, as young working stiffs, they never experienced true adolescence—rather, they began to experience it only as adults, once they got hold of leisure time in the late 1960s. As leisured, moneyed twenty-somethings, they began to rebel in a very adolescent way against the establishment in ways they never could have when life depended on passing a BBC audition or selling shows to the manager of some regional ballroom. This rebellion was free-floating and extended even into their own inner circle, to the point that they began belittling their well-meaning mentor George Martin.

Lennon, in particular, seemed to feel that he could not be outrageous enough. When subsequent proclamations failed to generate as much outrage as his "more popular than Christ" statement, Lennon pushed the envelope even more. In 1968, he and Yoko released a startling album titled *Two Virgins,* which comprised wild tape loops and strange noises. However, this was not the main reason the album was startling. The cover held the album's most notable feature (or features): photographs taken straight on of John and Yoko standing entirely nude before the camera. Remember—this was a man who proclaimed that he had come back from India to become a businessman.

If Lennon had snapped the pic and kept it as a private memento, it would have posed no problem from a business standpoint. Instead, he followed an adolescent whim—the equivalent of mooning someone from a passing car—to its logical (or illogical) conclusion. He mixed business and pleasure in a way that, like sardines and ice cream, was unpalatable to the marketplace. Lennon alienated multitudes of fans with this unimaginable (at the time) act.

Even today, nude photos of celebrities can have life-altering effects on their careers. Suppose someone in your organization circulated a photograph of him and his girlfriend in the nude. In today's Internet age, such a transgression is even easier. Could that ever be overcome? Don't find out. Make sure you keep adolescent behavior out of the workplace.

69

Disagreements and Conflict Resolution

Whenever two or more are gathered, there is a chance for disagreement. The longer the two are together, the more likely it becomes that there will be debate, especially among those who are creative and passionate. The question is not whether there will be conflict; it is how that conflict will be resolved, and at what cost.

The resolution of conflict is perhaps the most important ingredient in a partnership. Some sort of synthesis is almost always preferable to stalemate. If agreement is reached, both sides of the argument vanish. Keep in mind that all of the conflicting ideas may each have merit as stand-alone theories, as opposed to *this* is right, therefore *that* must be wrong. And, two disparate theories can inform one piece of work. The work is the thing to be preserved.

During the recording of "Ob-La-Di, Ob-La-Da," a McCartney song that John apparently detested, an inordinate amount of time was being spent in an attempt to create an introduction to the song. John was at his wit's end and, after several hours, stormed out of the session. He returned three or four hours later and screamed from the top of the stairway that led down into the studio, "I'm more stoned than any of you will ever be!" "Here's your intro!" he announced. He then descended the stairs to the piano and with all his might banged several chords upon the keyboard. All eyes shifted to Paul, expecting rejection, perhaps an outburst. "That's quite good, actually," he acknowledged. If you listen to "Ob-La-Di, Ob-La-Da" you will hear John's intro.

There you have it: John's stoned, almost ridiculous intro, conceived in a fit of pique, dramatically introduced the song in just the right way. Out of conflict—synthesis. The underlying disagreement about whether the song had merit in the broader scheme of things did not disappear, but resolving the conflict informed the work and made it stronger, rather than destroying it.

Another pitfall is wasting energy anticipating and preparing for a battle where none may unfold. For example, when Paul McCartney was writing "Hey Jude," he had written the line "don't carry the world upon your shoulders." Later in the song he included the line, "the movement you need is on your shoulder." When he played the song for John the first time and came to the latter line, anticipating criticism, he told John that he realized he had been repetitious with the word "shoulder" and that he needed to change the second line. John responded that he felt that the "movement you need is on your shoulder" was a great line, and that both lines should remain intact. In fact, he was adamant about it. Although Paul had planned for an argument and had a solution in mind, no argument ensued.

Disagreements will happen. Expect them, and allow them. But try not to waste energy second-guessing yourself, or placing your partners in adversarial positions prematurely. Remember the old biblical adage, "Sufficient unto each day is the evil thereof." Or Lennon-McCartney's more colloquial take on it, courtesy of Ringo, "Tomorrow never knows."

70
Becoming a Burden

At some point during the life of a company, one of the leaders can become a burden or albatross to the group—often unbeknownst to the albatross itself. John Lennon became an albatross for the Beatles. His relationship with Yoko Ono grew notorious, and the bizarre publicity that the couple intentionally generated damaged the group.

After the *Two Virgins* brouhaha, John and Yoko adopted the cause of world peace and began a series of "bed-ins," inspired by the early 1960s "sit-ins," which had brought attention to segregation in the United States. These "bed-ins" featured the two of them in pajamas talking of peace. Many journalists, perhaps hoping that more nudity was in the offing, would attend these bed-ins. They were disappointed. Needless to say, the amount of energy that Lennon had spent on the Beatles was now being allocated to other projects. Not only were these activities not beneficial to the group, they worked to the band's detriment in a number of ways and alienated untold multitudes of fans.

Although most companies would be hard pressed to find examples as dramatic as the Lennon-Ono capers, there are numerous ways you or your key players can drive off the cliff. Adultery, substance abuse, perhaps even something as mundane as using the company name to promote a private endeavor or controversial cause. Whatever the case, when a principal becomes a burden, the problem should be addressed immediately. Obviously, shifts of priority and attention away from the organization have taken place. The options are clear: The person ceases the questionable behavior, modifies it in a way that does not tarnish the company, or leaves.

The other Beatles, still young and perhaps wanting to appear hip or "with it," probably did not feel that they could issue such an ultimatum to John. Perhaps they also feared for their livelihoods. After all, their financial situation, individually and collectively, was still relatively perilous. And it was hard to imagine the Beatles without John.

By taking a wait-and-see attitude, the Beatles were still able to give us one more fine album and one classic, *Let It Be* and *Abbey Road,* respectively. In retrospect, we'll cut them some slack. We should thank them, in a way, for what their suffering gave us. But the remaining three might have had fewer emotional issues about the breakup of the Beatles if they had booted John out on his arse when he started to treat them shabbily and misbehave so publicly. It might have been worth it—to them.

And maybe—just maybe—this accountability would have served to temper John's emotions and behavior and create a new reserve of respect—which he now clearly lacked—for the others. Lennon would have been forced to address head-on whether or not the Beatles meant anything to him, instead of killing them slowly with a thousand paper cuts. Maybe a new working relationship—looser, but still based on mutual goodwill—could have developed between the Beatles and their tormented, brilliant, and reluctant leader. Maybe.

71

Gangster Management

In Mario Puzo's *The Godfather,* perhaps the most famous concept is the idea of making someone "an offer he can't refuse." The figure of Don Corleone is a compelling one. Who hasn't wanted a tough guy in his corner, making the opposition an offer they can't refuse? Beware!

A strong organized crime presence has long been associated with the music industry. Even if this were not the case, certain affinities would still exist between the music industry and the Mafia. One might pun that they are both hit-driven. They share the profit motive of traditional businesses, yet they tolerate or even encourage behaviors that have no place in staid organizations. Their profits depend not on the educational background, grooming, or even the intelligence of the people participating, but on one essential proposition—the "offer" we can't refuse—whether it be a hit song or the palpable threat of bodily harm. (Think about it—you would buy a hit song by someone whose derelict countenance you might otherwise cross the street to avoid. But you probably wouldn't buy anything else from him. Unless, of course, he threatened to break your thumbs!)

Perhaps this sense of being "outside" is why musicians are particularly prone to the romance of the gangster. Many musicians during the late 1960s and early 1970s had the misfortune to be associated with what Joey Molland (of Badfinger)—whose manager kept all of the band's millions—refers to as "gangster managers." Although not actual gangsters, men like Allen Klein cultivated an air of bluntness, informality, and even danger that appealed to musicians bored or frustrated with the more straitlaced corporate types at their labels.

John Lennon had heard from Mick Jagger that Klein, a New York tough guy revered for squeezing money out of recalcitrant record labels, had been able to get the Stones a better record deal than the Beatles had with their label. Lennon decided that Klein was just the man to sort out the mess at Apple. George and Ringo immediately agreed with John, while Paul wanted his in-laws, Lee and John Eastman, to represent the Beatles as they moved forward. After much squabbling, McCartney was voted down (in Beatle tradition) three to one. It is easy to see how the other Beatles may have mistrusted the idea of Paul's father-in-law representing all four Beatles equally. Yet their choice—the gangster manager—was arguably no better.

Klein won some big victories for the band, including an unprecedented royalty rate. As a band, the Beatles fared better than some of Klein's other clients like the Stones, who lost almost everything to Klein, including the rights to their classic music, basically having to start over. However, like a silent Mafia "partner" in a restaurant, Klein soon began to "bust out" the Beatles, violating artistic and musical integrity—the cornerstone of their success—in exchange for immediate cash to line their (and his) pockets. In part, this was a by-product of how he was incentivized. Klein's pitch—that he should only be paid for increased revenue—had initially appealed to Lennon, but it gave Klein a kind of laser focus on maximizing revenue (to the exclusion of artistic goals) that put him on a collision course with McCartney and eventually would help kill the golden goose.

Part of the royalty deal involved allowing the record company to repackage and reissue Beatle music; a key aspect of controlling the band's musical legacy was now out of their control. (Predictably, there was a flood of ill-conceived compilations in the 1970s.) Klein also pushed through the Phil Spector doctored *Let It Be* album, which McCartney considered distinctly subpar for the Beatles. Klein seemed to view the Beatles as a cash cow, a perspective which did not endear him to McCartney. Worse, because of a ten-year partnership agreement entered into in 1967, McCartney would essentially be "in bed" with Klein until 1977. He eventually found the arrangement unacceptable for numerous reasons and sued for the dissolution of the partnership in 1970.

Steer clear of the gangsters in your world. They are charming, they are tough, they have many qualities we admire. They may even produce some short-term results for you, but long-term, they are looking out for themselves only, and your business will suffer. The bottom line: if you enlist a gangster, the only person certain to benefit is the gangster. There is a good reason why established, successful businesses are somewhat staid and predictable. It works!

72
Bailing Out On Bad Financial Investments

There is a dark, nasty, painful side to running a business. One of the most painful things that one can do is to admit failure, count one's losses, release employees, and move on. Some men are born for this role. None of the Beatles was such a man, but Allen Klein was. Immediately upon taking office as the Beatles' manager, he closed Apple Films, Zapple, Apple Retail, and Apple Foundation for the Arts. He fired a number of longtime Apple employees, many of whom may, in truth, have preferred unemployment to working under Klein.

The closure of these failed enterprises, with their losses in the millions, was well reported and to this day the Beatles are widely viewed as business failures. The Apple "debacle" lives on in infamy in the popular imagination; what most recall about the company is its rather spectacular flame-out. The truth is that Apple is alive and well and quite profitable. In fact, the surviving Beatles (and the heirs of John and George) continue to own one of the most successful record companies in the world. The greatest asset of a record label is its talent. Apple already had the Beatles, of course. Add Badfinger, James Taylor, and the solo works of John Lennon, McCartney, George Harrison, and Ringo Starr to the roster, and it is difficult to top.

The purge at Apple left a huge black eye on the "peace and love" aspect of the Beatles' myth and put the lie to the quaint idea of a cottage industry run along the lines of "Western Communism." But for better or worse, it put the slimmer, sleeker company firmly back on the road to profitability, a road it has traveled now well into its *fifth* decade. (That's not a misprint.)

In the young century, as we see banks and manufacturers swept away or changed forever, it is important to remember that change is the lifeblood of business. At some point, underperforming assets must be dealt with. If you don't choose to deal with them, the marketplace will eventually choose the time and place for you. And it doesn't suffer fools gladly. Whatever you fear may happen if you take action, you can be sure it will be worse if you don't.

So, if you've got some assets or personnel that are weighing you down and need to go, channel your inner Allen Klein. Admit your failures. Count your losses. Liquidate the offending assets. Fire the offending personnel. And don't forget to move on.

73
Politics

If you are a business owner, you should be aware of the activities of local, state, and federal governments from the get-go. For the entrepreneurial personality, this can be a challenge. The slow-moving wheels of government are not very interesting. Moreover, entrepreneurial personalities tend to view all obstacles as impermanent and surmountable. The problem is, often nothing is more permanent than government policy, regulation, or intervention, particularly with regard to taxation.

Consider how Lloyd George destroyed the Beatles, aided and abetted by Harold Wilson. From previous chapters we know that the Beatles were basically goaded into starting the Apple group of companies as a way of "sticking it to the man"—to avoid paying 90 percent of their cash reserves straight into Her Majesty's Treasury.

Without this potent tax dilemma, it is doubtful that Apple would have been founded—at least, not in the cash-sucking and energy-sucking form that it was. And without the eventual Apple mess to clean up, there would have been no point of entry for Allen Klein. Without Allen Klein, there would have been no split between the three other Beatles and Paul. In short, though they probably wouldn't have lasted forever, like the Stones, the Beatles would likely have behaved more rationally—and lasted longer—under a more rational tax burden.

These punitive tax policies were the work of Lloyd George, a World War I–era British prime minister. And though none of the Beatles was likely pondering tax policy as they began their ascent, the British government was lying in wait for them—in a very real sense it saw them coming a mile away. Lloyd George may have set the trap, but a second prime minister, Harold Wilson, further set the boys up by nominating them for acceptance into the Most Excellent Order of the British Empire in 1965, perhaps mindful of their impact on the British balance of trade. By accepting this honor from the Queen, the boys may have effectively taken the best tax remedies, such as leaving the country or setting up foreign corporations, off the table. Whereas the Stones had no problem eventually leaving the country and forming a series of Dutch corporations to handle their affairs, the Beatles—members of the Order of the British Empire all—took their lumps, eventually imploding from the stress.

The moral of the story? Government law, regulations, and policy can destroy your company at a whim. This is true for longstanding policies, like the British super tax, but also for sudden changes in law or policy. So, be on your toes! Not to denigrate paying your fair share of taxes, but keep in mind that preserving what you have built—including the jobs you are providing and the longevity of the government's tax base—may entail radical and strategic solutions. Remember, if you go out of business, the government gets nothing!

The second moral of the story is that political entanglements and affiliations can be costly—whether they are pro- or anti-authoritarian. Though John Lennon is more commonly remembered for alienating fans with his sometimes controversial anti-authoritarian, pacifist, and atheist views, his most costly alliance—in terms of earnings—may well have been his early alignment with Her Majesty's government as an MBE.

74
Me Against Them

As the old saying goes, just because you are paranoid doesn't mean they are not out to get you. Unlike the old days, when it was "I am he as you are he as you are me and we are all together," by late 1968, Paul McCartney was becoming increasingly isolated from the other Beatles. We have touched in previous chapters on John Lennon's diminishing interest—for various reasons—in taking a leadership role in the Beatles. As this happened, McCartney, already first among equals, began to step more and more into the breach.

But though none of the Beatles seemed to express resentment of John, their trouble-prone, absentee leader—for his nudity, bed-ins, Bagism, involvement with the peace movement, solo concerts, and recordings with his new Plastic Ono Band, or any of the other many distractions that kept him from focusing on their common livelihood—slowly but surely they began to resent McCartney for his well-intended, if slightly controlling, efforts on their behalf. There could be several reasons for this. All the other Beatles, understandably, had begun to have interests apart from the group. Understandable, that is, to everyone but Paul McCartney. Gifted with a tremendous work ethic, he had always compressed his many extracurricular interests—in painting, filmmaking, and other avant-garde artistic pursuits—into his spare time. He also took great care to integrate his personal life, including his near engagement to Jane Asher, and budding relationship with Linda Eastman, neatly into his professional life. It is likely that he expected the others—perhaps reasonably, given the size and scale of the enterprise that they had created together—to do the same. The Beatles remained always at the center of his life.

Second, for better or worse, Paul McCartney did not intimidate the other Beatles the way John Lennon did. He did not have an easy hand at the rudder, but he also sought a greater degree of consensus than Lennon had. Ironically, this opened the door for criticism and resentment, especially from Harrison, that Lennon would never have tolerated. McCartney had firm ideas about the way things should be, but he also wanted to be liked, in some ways a problematic combination of traits for a leader.

The split began to manifest itself in many ways. John Lennon, George Harrison, and Ringo Starr all voted to hire Alan Klein as their manager, with McCartney voting solo for his in-laws, the

Eastmans. Paul's recurring idea of returning to live performance—which he alone had missed since their last concert in 1966—was repeatedly shot down, in the unkindest of terms, by the others.

In any group of more than two people, there will be occasions when one person takes one side of an issue and all the others oppose that view. As long as it varies issue to issue as to which person stands alone, this can be a healthy dynamic. When a pattern develops such that the same person is fighting against the group issue after issue, however, a serious problem has emerged.

As mentioned in chapter 70, the Beatles probably should have called it quits at this point, handing John Lennon his walking papers for nonparticipation, or even, arguably, deliberate sabotage. But even the overtly bored and hostile Lennon balked at destroying the group so soon after signing a new contract, and a lucrative one at that. In the parlance of the twenty-first century, perhaps on some level they all felt that the Beatles were "too big to fail." And McCartney, to his credit, through some combination of persistence, luck, and perhaps a bit of denial, managed to steer the group through one more great album, *Abbey Road.*

If you are in a dysfunctional partnership, look around. Don't be afraid to make hard decisions—like leaving, or firing troublemakers, or even dissolving while your goodwill in the industry or community is intact. Trust your gut. Is there an *Abbey Road* left in your enterprise? Or are you a "zombie" company—dead, but you just don't know it yet?

75

Taking Control

When the company begins a downward spiral, someone must take control. That person must have the best interests of the company as top priority, and the welfare of the members as a secondary focus. However, there are limits to what that person can accomplish if he attempts to manufacture a return to the good old days, especially from the top down. *Esprit de corps* must come from shared goals, and new circumstances call for new ways of working—and new ways of leading.

In Liverpool, as Badfinger's Joey Molland has noted, the band had always been the thing: a unit, inseparable. But by January 1969, Paul could see the Beatles slipping away. John had Yoko, Ringo his acting career, and George, his devotion to a newfound religion. In an effort to bring the band together, Paul began to float the idea that returning to their roots would revive their flagging spirits and interest, and rekindle the friendship and camaraderie that they had enjoyed before. He tried to persuade them to play live as they had in Hamburg and the Cavern. That failed. He then decided to have them play live in the studio. The concept of the film *Let It Be* and its accompanying album was to write and produce songs quickly—as in "the old days"—and then to perform them, if only for the camera.

Nevermind that the Beatles' greatest accomplishment to date had been their swift, incredible, and unprecedented musical and lyrical progression from the novice Merseybeat albums such as *Please, Please Me,* moving rapidly through mid-period gems like *Revolver,* enhanced by increasingly sophisticated studio trickery and the judicious use of new and unusual musical textures, and finally to late-period masterpieces like *Sgt. Pepper* and *The White Album,* in which they bent whole orchestras, and seemingly the whole world, to their supple whims.

Paul found out the hard way you can't go home again, or get back to where you once belonged. Eight days into the session, George quit. Harrison had matured musically, and Paul—the overweening big brother figure—could do no right by him. The slightest instruction—or suggestion—from Paul set him off. There was open rebellion, and for the second time in as many albums—disregarding *Yellow Submarine*—a Beatle had quit. The entire, sad event was recorded on film. Ironically, Paul's notion of filming a return to the carefree days of yore caught instead the disintegration of the band and somehow effectively foreshadowed the encroaching gloom of the hairy, beige, dispirited 1970s, with their persistent political conflicts, gas shortages, scandals, stagflation, and pronounced lack of Beatles.

Paul, by badgering the others into making the film, and by offering numerous suggestions to George, and in a thousand other ways, was, as a good leader should be, operating for the good of the enterprise. He may have been seeking in good faith to lead by example, but unwilling or unable to accommodate ways of working outside his own comfort zone, while simultaneously asking for the others to stretch outside theirs, he dominated the proceedings, pushed his partners away, and brought the business into further disarray.

76
Recruiting

During the life of any business entity, there come periodic doldrums, where inspiration, enthusiasm, and creativity are dulled by routine. Ironically, the very parameters that defined success can come to feel restrictive. After a prolonged relationship of any kind, people become so familiar with their partners that they know what their next move will be, even to completing their sentences. They tire of their jokes, the repetition of their jargon, and the consistency of certain quirks. Tempers may flare and personal relationships fray around the edges as people tire of the same old faces and the same old ways of doing things.

In times like these, one solid strategy is to recruit new blood. It's just human nature. Someone new around the conference table puts everyone on their best behavior. To set the old adage on its ear, unfamiliarity breeds respect, or at least civility. It provides a breather, pushes the reset button, and clears the stage for new energy and ideas.

It is especially essential in a creative environment to incorporate new personalities that can inspire. During the recording of *The White Album*, after the studio had filled with anger and sarcasm, George brought Eric Clapton, widely considered at that point the finest blues and rock guitarist in the world, into the studio. Harrison felt that the others would behave themselves if they had visitors. And, they did. Clapton became the first outside "name" in the pop world—the first outsider famous in his own right—to play on a Beatle release.

But Clapton brought more than a calming influence into the studio. He brought his talent and his musical genius to inspire and uplift George. "While My Guitar Gently Weeps" was George's best composition to date, but Clapton's winding, sinewy solo—heavily processed with characteristic Beatle-style studio effects—took it to another level entirely. In essence, Clapton made his sponsor in the Beatle world look like a genius by creating stellar work that had been heretofore impossible.

Later, when the atmosphere in the studio during *Let It Be* became unbearable, George returned again, this time with Billy Preston, a keyboard player whose gleeful presence and wide, sweeping gap-toothed smile brought a spark to the group. Preston's solo on "Get Back" is the best keyboard work on a Beatles record. It made the song. Had he not been recruited, the songs recorded might have been too disastrous for release. Again, kudos to Harrison.

It is worth noting that George Harrison, the second banana, the "little brother" Beatle, the odd man out, seemed to understand this better than John and Paul, who, because they felt such closely held ownership of all things "Beatle" in their minds, never thought of sharing their work with major talents like Clapton and Preston. Harrison demonstrated the same genius for casting and the initiative that enabled him in the 70s to record his sprawling three-record masterpiece, *All Things Must Pass*, with dispatch.

In any endeavor, at some point, survival is based on the nourishment of the body—whether it is new capital or new ideas, or just new faces. When you tire of the same old same old, step back and mix it up a little. Seek the advice of your George Harrisons, your underutilized geniuses-in-waiting. Only with different stimuli will different results come.

77
Diversity

There is another lesson to be drawn from the events of the preceding chapter, in which George Harrison had the insight and dynamism to bring in Eric Clapton and later Billy Preston to improve both the work product and the interpersonal dynamics of his workplace. That lesson is an awareness of the benefits of diversity.

The Beatles were products of their era, in which diversity itself had yet to be articulated as an end in itself. They tended to display a sort of cheerful chauvinism in many areas of life—for better or worse, they worked in what amounted to a very exclusive "boys only" club. However, as time wore on, they demonstrated a very forward-thinking mentality, particularly in their personal lives. John, of course, defied a certain amount of ethnophobia by taking a free-spirited, bohemian Japanese woman as his lover (eventually his wife) and his intellectual mentor. George's openness to an Eastern religion brought him spiritual happiness until the day he died.

None of these developments was particularly reassuring to the marketplace, or to the Beatles' fans, who may have been unsettled by the increasing "otherness" of the Beatles' world, as evidenced by the droning sitars, Eastern philosophy, and nine-minute excursions into *music concrete* that began to crop up as Beatle songs. Not to mention the increasingly bizarre personal antics of John in particular.

The melding of a diverse group of individuals into a single unit produces a whole that is indeed greater than the sum of its parts. The right combination can lead to an indivisible, invincible force, like the Beatles, at least at the beginning. Yet, it is now considered axiomatic that no partnership—no enterprise—can expand creatively without diversity. Ideally, there should be an ethnic, sexual, religious, political, and socioeconomic mix in order to bring new ideas and philosophies into the mind and soul of the partnership.

After all, it took the gospel-flavored stylings of Billy Preston, an African American, to save *Let It Be*. It took Yoko Ono to give John a new lease on life in the Beatles and beyond. And it took the Hare Krishna mantra to finally get George Harrison to number one with "My Sweet Lord." In the spirit of the day, even the most apolitical Beatle—Paul—worked sly allusions to the American civil rights movement into his famous "Blackbird."

Some of these accomplishments were to be built on the ashes of the Beatles, to be sure. In at least one area, the fans were correct:

the core of "otherness" in the Beatles may have helped to sow the seeds of the eventual dissolution of the group, as George and John grew increasingly disaffected with the lifestyle available to them as a Beatle. Unfortunately—or fortunately, the alternatives may well have been worse. Would we rather have *Plastic Ono Band* and *All Things Must Pass,* or John and George singing along dispiritedly on "Uncle Albert/Admiral Halsey"? Eventually, the diverse ideas and perspectives yielded multiple masterpieces, none of which could be said to be very similar to the others.

As the case history of the Beatles shows, there are risks to diversity. No organization can be all things to all people. Diversity may ultimately splinter your enterprise, or create dynamic new offshoots that thrive and prosper, maybe even at your expense. But the alternative is stagnation and, just as surely, failure.

Don't be afraid to take the measure of your organization against all of humankind. As theologian Paul Tillich once wrote, "Doubt is an essential element in an act of faith." Only after others bring into question the opinions and beliefs that a person feels to be true, and those theories are revised, dismissed, or reaffirmed, can true faith be attained. And only then can the true potential of that individual—or company—be achieved.

78
Depression

Depression can creep into lives in many different ways—from chemical abuse, physical pain, or mental strain. It can be purely situational. In whatever form, it is not only painful for the person suffering from depression. It is also damaging to personal and professional relationships. Once depression invades your life, or the life of your organization, your first priority should be to adopt a successful strategy to beat it. Wage all-out war against it. It's a question of survival, because depression can kill you—and your company.

Looking now at the Beatles' *Let It Be* movie, it is clear that the Beatles, grungy a full two decades before Kurt Cobain, were suffering from various forms and degrees of depression. Humor, once

a Beatles trademark, was in short supply, though not completely absent. There was quite a bit of poor playing, arguments, and
pointless, meandering conversation. The overall energy level was,
mildly put, low.

Yet the old magic was not completely gone. After all, they were
working. Longtime Beatles associate Tony Bramwell has said that
the Beatles were "postwar working-class people [who] worked every day and took two weeks off for holiday." Indeed, there was an
almost blue-collar mentality afoot when the band was at its peak.
Once in the studio, in their element, they could not help developing a sense of flow and getting lost in the work. Engineer Geoff
Emerick has noted that when he would enter the studio floor to
position microphones around Ringo's kit, the floor would often
be littered with wood chips. These wood chips were fragments of
Ringo's drumsticks, which splintered as a result of the other Beatles
constantly exhorting him to hit the drums harder. Yes, the Beatles
liked to work, and work hard.

The rooftop concert is perhaps the most famous example of
when the magic was working. McCartney's idea of returning to
live work, no matter how briefly, had always met with resistance
and even open derision. Yet once they were there, in the moment,
with the cameras rolling, the spirit of the early Beatles emerged
and towered over London, as if they had rubbed a magic lamp.
John Lennon's humor even returned, and his closing remark, "I'd
like to say thank you on behalf of the group and ourselves and I
hope we passed the audition," has passed into legend. It also serves
as evidence of how effectively McCartney's stratagem resurrected,

however fleetingly, the spirit of their early days, when they had something to prove.

Given what we know now, this is actually not very surprising. Research has shown that your physiology and your emotions are intimately liked, and energy flows both ways. In other words, we smile when we are feeling good, but we can also make ourselves feel better by smiling. This is essentially what McCartney accomplished on that rooftop—the physicality of playing the show actually made the Beatles happier, however briefly.

If your people are in a funk, don't hesitate to consult a psychologist. But you may want to try one or two Beatles-style remedies in the interim. Take them back to a time (and possibly a place) when you all were busier, happier, and more productive. Remind them of the times when everything was ticking over. Help them "fake it till they make it." Then start looking around for those wood chips!

79

Self-evaluation

By July 1969, if Paul had performed a candid evaluation of his band, he would have realized—and perhaps he did realize—that even with the rooftop performance during *Let It Be,* the Beatles were more than likely finished. They were too fractured to heal. There is no reason why it had to be so. A quick study of what remained of the four lads from Liverpool would have revealed that the talent was there, more developed artistically, stylistically, musically, and lyrically. They were all better writers, singers, and had a better understanding of record production, even as the technology had advanced.

And yet, within the inner circle, defections and rebellions large and small were common. The Beatles had lost Geoff Emerick. During *The White Album* sessions, Ringo had briefly departed. During *Let It Be,* George quit the group. The other George, George Martin, was also by mutual agreement, absent from the session. It seemed that at any one time, a quorum of those responsible for the Beatles' greatest successes were missing in action, and those still fighting could barely tolerate the sight of one another. Surely Paul and John knew that George was seething—but were unwilling or unable to use that information to correct their own behavior that was contributing to the situation.

The key to preventing this kind of situation is candid, and timely, self-evaluation by the leaders of the enterprise. Just as you know where those last few pounds you need to lose are lurking, or where the last vestige of clutter is in your home, you probably know where the developing problems in your business are. You probably just don't like to think about it, preferring to focus on the more immediate concerns. To some extent, it is coded into human nature to neglect long-term threats, even when they are potentially catastrophic. We focus on the urgent, and neglect the all-important.

If this is you, one day you could jump into making your next "album" only to find your whole business going up in flames. Right now, problems in your company are staring you in the face. Don't wait for the autopsy to see what you should have done. Evaluate the situation and address the problem now.

80
Be What You Are (Were)

It is always nice to go out a winner, but it doesn't always happen that way. Partnerships, bands, companies, friends, even armies disintegrate. So if it happens, roll with it. Start anew. Leaving one situation and going to another need not be defeat. In Major League baseball, there are numerous instances in which managers are fired from one team and hired by another team with a dismal record, only to lead that new team to the World Series. It happens in most professional sports. The coaches do not change their techniques or philosophies; rather, the new team responds better.

The same often happens in music. Some musicians, like Eric Clapton, build a career out of leap-frogging. You can trace his lineage from the Yardbirds to John Mayall and the Bluesbreakers, to

Cream, to a one-gig stint with the Plastic Ono Band, then on to Blind Faith, Derek and the Dominos, and a long and varied solo career. Acknowledging his motley career, Clapton even called his 1989 album *Journeyman.*

The problem is that it was not supposed to happen to the Beatles. But by 1969, five short years after *The Ed Sullivan Show,* but a lifetime to their fans, there were rumblings of a breakup. The "Say it ain't so, Joes" were hoping and praying that it would not happen, but the Beatles seemed to know it was over. Remarkably, they summoned the willpower, energy, and focus to go out winners with one last masterpiece. Paul McCartney did not want it to end with the mess that was *Let It Be.* With the understanding that they could not self govern, he contacted George Martin and asked him to produce another record.

Martin, himself, had reassessed his life and decided that there was life after the Beatles, although he, too, wanted a swan song. He agreed to produce the record if they would agree to do it the old way, with him giving direction. Paul assured him that the others had agreed. The result was *Abbey Road,* one of their best albums. There are numerous suggestions that they knew it was their last. Geoff Emerick noted that he thought the album cover photograph with them walking away from Abbey Road studios was chosen by the group for its symbolism; there had been several shots of them walking toward the studio.

This album helped launch the solo career of an unlikely Beatle as George Harrison scored his first A-side single with his composition "Something," a song that rivals "Yesterday" for the most covers or re-recordings by other artists. His song "Here Comes the Sun" opened the second side of the record and has become a standard. George Harrison had established himself as a songwriter of the first rank. Tellingly, the second side of the album contains a medley of songs, some written by Lennon, others by McCartney, since there had been no joint compositions in several years. At the end of the medley, there was a place for an extended guitar solo. Emerick feels that the way in which they prepared for this work is the final proof that they knew it was over.

At this point, there were three Beatles who were accomplished and distinctive soloists on the guitar. The plan was that Paul, who had written that part of the medley, would solo first, then George, the nominal lead guitarist, would come next, and finally, John would add some rough and ready business in conclusion. They would then repeat that pattern until the solo section had ended.

The three of them went down into the studio to record the work together, something they had not done in recent years. As had been the practice for some time, Yoko followed John and was walking with him into the studio. Emerick recalls that John stopped her at the door, and said, "Not this time, Love." With that gracious gesture, the Beatles were Beatles again for one last song.

81
Gimmickry and Fools

Incredibly, there was a new and strange development—a marketing campaign of sorts—that breathed new life into the Beatles' record sales at the same time the Beatles as a group were dying. However, had this campaign been proposed to the group or its management, it would most certainly have been rejected as insane.

Following the release of *Abbey Road,* a disk jockey in Detroit announced that the album cover contained clues pointing to the fact that Paul McCartney was dead. Among the "clues" was the fact that in the cover photograph, the four Beatles are crossing the street and Paul is barefooted, a suggestion that he is prepared for burial, while George, in his blue jeans and work shirt, represented the gravedigger, Ringo in his black suit the mortician, and John in his dress whites, the priest.

Additionally, Paul is out of step from the other three, and a Volkswagen parked on the side of the road has the license plate 28IF suggesting that McCartney would be 28 years of age were he alive. Conspiracy theorists found additional fodder for their ideas on three other Beatles albums. When the words "Number Nine" that are included in the song "Revolution #9" on *The White Album* are played backward, they appear to say "Turn me on dead man." (Oddly enough, that is true.) There are also numerous clues in the materials inside the *Sgt. Peppers Lonely Hearts Club Band* album—including speculation that "A Day in the Life" tells the story of the fatal car wreck that claimed Paul's life—and the insert and cover of the *Magical Mystery Tour* album. Here's the kicker: in order to research all of the death clues, a Beatles fan would need to purchase all four albums—the albums recorded after Paul's "death." This hoax caused the Beatles' album sales to skyrocket to Beatlemania proportions. Had it been part of a deliberate marketing plan, it would have been (even more) legendary.

As your company succeeds, it too will draw the crazies. The scary thing is, they may be on to something. You will become a magnet for the bizarre, unpredictable creativity of the group mind. This effect is accelerated in the Internet age, and many companies seek purposely to manufacture, or at least ride the wave of, "viral" ideas.

When contemplating your personal "Paul is dead" moment, be careful to think long-term. Before entering into any type of arrangement, it should be ascertained that there is no conflict of interest, and that promotion of the new venture or concept will not damage the reputation of the company. Remember that there has never been anything that could link the Beatles to having participated in or orchestrated the "Paul is dead" hoax; if there had been a link, it would have tarnished their legacy. Don't let attention to the trend of the moment cheapen the long-term value of your work.

82

Game Face

With *Abbey Road* recorded and ready for release, Paul McCartney's breakup nightmare was fast becoming reality: John Lennon now informed the other Beatles that he was officially leaving the group. But Lennon told almost no one else. To the outside world, the Beatles were, for all intents and purposes, a working group with a new album about to come out.

To recap, Ringo had left temporarily during *The White Album*, George temporarily during *Let It Be*, and John permanently following *Abbey Road*. Yet none of these incidents was common knowledge until years later. The reasons all boil down to money. Allen Klein was in the process of renegotiating the Beatles' royalties on their previously released albums as well as albums yet to come, such as *Abbey Road* and *Let It Be* (which, though recorded in 1968, would not be released until 1970).

As badly as some of the band might have wanted to shout from the rooftops that they were free at last, they had to hold it under wraps so as not to weaken Klein's leverage. The tactic worked and the Beatles' royalties increased immensely. Some might argue that this gambit was disingenuous or even dishonest. It seems out of character especially for John, who cultivated an image of blunt honesty and, at that time, effected a take-it-or-leave-it attitude about money.

For all his bluster, in this instance, Lennon's reserve spared the Beatles—and ultimately his own estate—the unnecessary loss of additional royalties from the hard work that had consumed the young adulthood of these four men. Had the announcement of the impending breakup been made public, the Beatles—and their heirs—would still be paying the price. In this, he showed extraordinary foresight and fortitude.

When any company begins to falter, the vultures begin to circle. In many cases, when companies have been in weak, yet easily correctable, financial condition, the very prophecy of their failure causes their demise. Creditors become more aggressive, sometimes forcing bankruptcy on companies that could have pulled through. Negotiations stall. In cases of publicly traded companies, there have been examples when loose lips have wrecked deals altogether or cost shareholders millions of dollars.

As Don Corleone said in the *Godfather*, "Never tell anybody outside the family what you are thinking." John didn't.

83
Greed

Greed—the narrow and myopic focus on personal gain—is a disease that cannot be allowed to infiltrate your decision-making. Ultimately, the survival of your business depends on providing something of value to your customers or clients and not on the maximization of your own profit. If you have read this far, you probably know this already. Unfortunately, greed can still attack your business from the outside.

The Beatles acted in good faith when they signed with their publisher, Dick James, accepting a standard industry contract, albeit one that favored the publisher. The publishing contract had only been in place a short time when they became very successful. It was apparent that the publisher would not be forced to perform the duties normally associated with a publisher-writer relationship, such as recording demos, pitching songs, negotiating contracts with record labels, and so forth, yet he would still reap all the traditional rewards. Amazingly, James never really saw the problem here.

James started a new publishing company just for the Beatles called Northern Songs. John and Paul each owned a percentage as did Brian Epstein. After the Beatles enjoyed their early success, James took the company public, thereby reducing the ownership of John and Paul, but including George and Ringo at a small percentage. James himself retained the largest percentage. As the Beatles did well, the company prospered, increasing in value by more than 400 percent.

Perhaps not surprisingly, Dick James sold his shares at a huge profit without telling the Beatles, and to this day they have never been able to buy back a controlling interest in the publishing rights for their own songs. This means they have no control over whether their songs are used in commercials or films, and also means that they do not receive that share of the income from radio play and other uses. (It should be noted that the canny Harrison, whose songs did not start appearing on Beatles' records until later, avoided this pitfall, beginning his own publishing company, Harrisongs, in 1968.)

The lesson? If you are dependent upon an ancillary company, even if the relationship is good, make sure that the other company is aware that you would like the opportunity to buy—if it ever sells. Have an attorney prepare a "right of first refusal" contract with important vendors so that they cannot act against your interests without your knowledge. Keep in mind that many times, the sale of the company is not being considered, but another company appears out of nowhere and makes the management an offer that the company cannot refuse. Therefore, in day-to-day affairs, beware the greedy. The same logic applies among the partners or principals in any entity: they should have a buy-sell agreement in case greed walks in the door and pits partner against partner.

A further caveat: if there is one in the group who is clearly susceptible to greed, do not let that person negotiate on behalf of the group. Although it would seem that this person would be able to secure the best deal, such grabbiness often backfires. If the other side smells a rat, they will walk away, never to return to the table. Trying to squeeze the last drop of blood from a deal can kill it.

In summary, greed is *not* good. Practice enlightened self-interest, for the good of your business and of your soul.

84
Limbo

It is likely that anyone who has switched jobs has experienced a period of limbo between jobs. Perhaps you know the feeling: the interviews for the new job were clandestine, and there is a constant, almost paralyzing paranoia that the current employer will learn of your intention to leave before the details of the new position have been agreed to.

The Beatles maintained the secrecy of their breakup in order to reap a better record royalty deal, all agreeing to lie low during the negotiations. George and Ringo's respective resignations had come and gone, but John's announcement that he wanted a "divorce" from the group was devastating. They knew that he intended to go through with it. And with no John Lennon, there would be no Beatles. The Beatles were in limbo.

The thing to do in limbo is to prepare to depart as soon as the time is right and not a moment sooner—or later. And so it was with John, George, and Ringo. John almost immediately began tipping his hand with releases by the Plastic Ono Band. George and Ringo began to plan their solo records, and George produced outside artists such as Doris Troy, Jackie Lomax, and Billy Preston. For John, George, and Ringo, their work with the Beatles became in some ways a long apprenticeship for their own signature efforts.

The person leaving limbo should—within the bounds of legality and ethical behavior—glean any appropriate information that may be useful in the new endeavor. One should hope that the new position or endeavor is a natural extension of the last, so that the same skill set can be used to hit the ground running with the same or better opportunities and results. Along the way, it should be a priority that no bridges are burned. For three of the Beatles, it was so: Ringo's most successful songs were written or produced by George. Ringo and George would play on Lennon's *Imagine* album.

Of the Beatles, perhaps Paul stayed in limbo the longest, though eventually he would emerge with a vengeance and continue to create brilliant pop music (perhaps the most convincing rebuttal to the "Paul is dead" claims). In fact, Paul would later have a television show titled "One Hand Clapping." Perhaps his time in limbo inspired the title, since he was the only Beatle still "in uniform," rearranging the deck chairs on a sinking ship. There was precious little applause for his pains.

85
Reincarnation

So you are out of limbo, freedom feels great, but now what? You're known as a top performer and that's what's expected of you and the pressure is on to deliver.

In September 1969, the Beatles released *Abbey Road*. In October, the Plastic Ono Band, consisting of John Lennon, Eric Clapton, Klaus Voormann, and Alan White, released the single "Cold Turkey." In November, John and Yoko released *The Wedding Album* and in December the Plastic Ono Band released *Live Peace In Toronto*. But the Beatles were still the Beatles.

As 1970 dawned, the Plastic Ono Band released the single "Instant Karma" in February, and the Beatles released the single "Let It Be" in March. Ringo released the album *Sentimental Journey* on

April 3, and Paul released *McCartney,* his first solo work on April 17, with the release of the album *Let It Be* in May. Ringo, that's right Ringo, released *Beaucoups of Blues,* his second solo album of the year in September, and George released his first solo album *All Things Must Pass* in November. Not to be outdone, John Lennon and the Plastic Ono Band released an eponymous album in December.

With the exception of Ringo, who would continue to improve, the body of work delivered by the emancipated solo artists was arguably as good as anything they had ever done, and song for song some of the best work they would ever accomplish. They had to be great again and they were. And then, the other shoe dropped. Paul, seething at some of the arrangements with Allen Klein, sued for dissolution of the group. Even then the public simply could not quite bring themselves to believe that the lads had broken up.

Even with history as a partner, attempting to understand how the world was unaware that the Beatles had disbanded after *Abbey Road,* even as all of the Beatle solo releases flooded the market, is problematic. In the days before our scandal-riddled present, perhaps there was more trust. If the Beatles said they were still together, then they must still be together, despite the persistent rumors.

But no one could now deny that Beatle John was now John Lennon, Beatle Paul was Paul McCartney, Beatle George was George Harrison, and Beatle Ringo was Ringo Starr. The endlessly fascinating four-cornered plaything of the imagination called the Beatles was broken. A little magic seemed to have gone out of the world, but the music remained.

86

Deconstruction, not Destruction

Even if key principals leave or the partners agree to end the partnership *per se,* the overarching corporate framework can persist, and prosper. The Beatles did not want to go forward as a band, but they wanted to write and record and they needed a publishing company (except for George, who had Harrisongs) and a record label to do so. Apple was there, and now devoid of its weirdness, it had the necessary infrastructure in place. This red-headed stepchild of the Beatle business model was about to enter its glory days. As a vehicle for the newly launched solo Beatle careers, it functioned admirably well. It still does to this day.

There are a number of ways to dismantle corporations, or partnerships, by the division of fixed assets as well as shares of ownership. As we have mentioned, it is much less troublesome to all if plans and provisions are made for this process during the inception of the enterprise, rather than trying to sort it all out at the end, when goodwill has been tested, grievances have been nurtured, and emotions have been running high. For partnerships in particular, the list of horrendous, lengthy court battles is much, much longer than the stories of clean, straightforward termination of the entity and liquidation of assets, or of seamless transitions to waiting successors.

Unfortunately, the end of the Beatles was messy—very messy. In the Beatles' dealings, it became another iteration of Paul against the other three. Perhaps the straw that broke the camel's back was their request that he delay the release of his solo album to avoid distracting from or competing with the release of *Let It Be,* the project he had initiated in an effort to restore band harmony, and during which the other Beatles—based on the filmed evidence—seemed to be intent on resisting or even sabotaging in one way or another.

They had made his life hell. Now, the other three, two of whom professed to embrace their newfound freedom, after all their recent solo recordings and concerts, were telling Paul he'd better delay his project for the sake of the dear old Beatles. It is not known how much of an ironist Paul McCartney is, but appreciating the irony would have been cold comfort—as was the lawsuit he filed shortly thereafter—dragging his three former buddies into court in an attempt to get them and Allen Klein out of his business, and finally let go of the dream.

87

Partners at War

The dynamics of breakups—be they marriages, partnerships, businesses, or friendships—can be most perplexing. The fact that people can live, work, play, share, struggle, and accomplish so much for so long with so little conflict, only to explode—or implode—later, is almost incomprehensible. Separation nevertheless comes more often than not. And sadly, in many cases, those deep bonds turn into equally deep divisions and animosity, and the partners find themselves despising each other and waging war.

Such was the case with John Lennon and his disdain for his former partner Paul McCartney, the other half of the best songwriting team in the world. These partners had achieved everything that a partnership could, except endurance. The one-sided feud was first observed following the release of *Ram,* Paul's second solo album, in May of 1971. The cover featured a photograph of Paul holding a ram by its horns. In October, John released his *Imagine,* which included a picture of him holding a pig by the ears, clearly lampooning McCartney's carefully selected rustic imagery. That dig may have been subtle, but the lyrics to the song "How Do You Sleep" were not. They included brutal lines dismissing McCartney's compositions as "Muzak" and claiming the "freaks" had been right when they said Paul was dead. (See chapter 81.)

Many have pondered why Lennon would hold McCartney—two men who had given each other and the world so much enjoyment with songs of love and peace—in such disdain. Some speculate that it was because of Paul's lawsuit, which, though it was "business," must certainly have affronted the other three Beatles personally. Whatever the case, Lennon was mad as hell and he waged his case in the court of public opinion. In hindsight, it might have been a better idea to keep the feud out of the public eye. Public conflicts force other people, in this case fans or customers, to take sides. Lennon may have lost thousands of fans with his song. Chances are, he didn't care.

While Lennon's lyrics are brutal, they are tame by comparison with things other business partners have said about each other in courtrooms and in the media. Most businesses and partnerships do not have the luxury of losing customers, or making them choose sides. Look around your conference table. Do you have the necessary buy-sell agreements in place? Can you—or your partners—get out of one another's airspace without going down in flames?

88
Philanthropy

It is never too late—or too early—to give back. Whether you are in your first year or your last, make a difference in the world of those who may never be able to do what you have done. They need you.

As you become recognized for your leadership abilities, more and more opportunities to apply those skills for the benefit of the universe will become available. Charities and causes can sniff out money and success and they need it; these nonprofits also recognize that they need leadership skills as well. The same skills that brought you this far can now be used in the service of others.

The good news is that involvement in these causes can improve the bottom line. You never know when you will meet your peers and competition—and even potential customers. There may be opportunities to form alliances in other, more lucrative areas. And good causes have a way of bringing people together for the long term. Perhaps this is why most successful business leaders—surely among the busiest people—are usually also found donating their time and expertise as volunteers.

You should be warned that one of the most popular forms of fundraising is the benefit—balls, soirees, concerts, festivals, or some other method of bringing people together to contribute to the cause. No doubt you will be asked to attend your fair share; you may come to dread these invitations, and the dry-cleaning bills for your tuxedo or evening gown.

When participating in these endeavors, make the effort to ensure that the funds flow into the right channels. George Harrison organized one of the first all-star charity concerts in 1971 in order to raise money for those who were starving as a result of cyclones and political unrest in Bangladesh. This concert was in response to a request from his friend and mentor Ravi Shankar. Although the event and subsequent album and film revenue raised millions of dollars, it took years to get most of the money out of various accounts, because of numerous tax and accounting problems. According to some, one of the primary holdups was that the organizers had failed to take the simple precaution of applying for tax-exempt status.

Prior to establishing a relationship with a charitable organization, do your due diligence. Otherwise, what starts as a public relations coup can turn into a black eye for your company. It is not difficult, for example, to review the nonprofit certification of an organization and to determine how much of the money raised actually benefits those in need. Having done that, prepare to do well by doing good. And dust off that tux.

89
Establishing Your Legacy

The Beatles and their estates have become very legacy-minded in recent years, particularly Sir Paul McCartney. Fortunately, despite their sometimes acrimonious post-breakup relationships, there is still far more to celebrate in the Beatles' legacy than to lament. And any overreaching by one—like trying to switch song credits from Lennon-McCartney to McCartney-Lennon—is promptly rebuffed by the others, and by those even more zealous guardians of the Beatles' legacy, their untold millions of fans.

Revisionist history rarely flies. History has a habit of being kinder to those who are honest about their limitations and mistakes. That being said, to some degree the future will treat your legacy as you direct. One of the best ways to ensure the accuracy of history's memory is to publish your memoirs. It is not necessary to wait until the end of your career to set it all down. After your initial successes, others will be interested almost immediately in how you accomplished what you did. The Beatles saw this early on and enlisted Hunter Davies to write their first authorized biography, a book titled simply *The Beatles,* published in 1968. By authorizing this work, they retained control of the content—and not incidentally, got paid for it.

A word of advice: most people think they can write because they can speak. However, hiring a professional writer will usually achieve better results than attempting to complete the task yourself. You may have considerable talent in your area of expertise, but the ability to tell a fascinating tale in nonfiction prose is challenging. If your writing style is not polished, your grand achievements may look ordinary and lame. Unfair, but true nonetheless. It's all in the presentation. You would not let a member of your group step outside her field of expertise for an important task, so don't do it yourself. Be careful with humor. Remember that without inflection or body language, your brilliant joke may be misunderstood and wreak havoc. Be discreet, and be truthful. Keep in mind that your writings can cause real harm to your personal relationships. When it is in black and white on the written page, it is permanent, and may outlive you and those you write about.

George Harrison wrote an autobiography and omitted much of John Lennon's contribution to his development. Lennon felt that he had spent years mentoring and tutoring George, and was reportedly deeply hurt by the omission. Before they could completely reconcile, John Lennon was assassinated.

90
Old Friends, New Deals

There are always a few viable business and investment opportunities that simply need some cash or some leadership to breathe life into them. But there are far more inane, impossible, or ill-considered schemes out there. Unfortunately, your friends are not apt to have a better track record than the average bear when distinguishing between the two.

Sooner or later, the knock will come at the door. It could be a close friend who has been supportive throughout the journey, but who has not approached you out of respect for your friendship. So it may be hard to say no, particularly if you're flush. But tread lightly. For every Tony Bramwell, who formed a profitable sideline by inventing the rock video while he worked for the Beatles, there is a Pete Shotton, an old Quarrymen mate of John Lennon's. Lennon funded Shotton's idea to open a grocery store. Although he kept it afloat for several years and reportedly repaid the loan, it eventually closed. It was a solid if unremarkable commercial venture, but supermarket retailing was hardly the best place for a Beatle to be investing his time, energy, or money. (Incidentally, Shotton would later head Apple Boutiques—which also failed.)

Keep in mind, too, that there is no need to solicit opportunities or ideas, as the Beatles did with Apple. That's just asking for trouble. Rest assured that they will come your way by virtue of your success. Remember Magic Alex Mardas, the self-proclaimed technological wizard who headed Apple's electronics division? "Recruited" by Apple's call for talent, he used hundreds of thousands of dollars to construct Apple Studios, which was to be a state-of-the-art, cutting-edge, high-tech, floating-on-air recording studio. After several years, it was still unfinished. Geoff Emerick stated that in order to make the studio functional after Alex's dismissal, it had to be completely dismantled and rebuilt, a total loss.

Remember, no one knows the secret ingredient to success. As John Lennon said, if the Beatles had known the secret of their own success they would have formed another group and become managers. Stay humble, stick to what you know, and be careful of old friends bearing new ideas.

91
Sex

During the interviews for this book, recording engineer extraordinaire Richard Dodd (the Traveling Wilburys, George Harrison, and scores of others) said that he felt "kiss and tell" memoirs or biographies all too often hurt the families of the subject and it should not matter to anyone who was having sex with whom unless having sex during a recording session helped the singer hit a particular note.

We agree, and for that reason, we won't parse the facts that the Beatles were four of the most famous and desirable young men in the world during the full flower of the "free love" era, or that their Hamburg apprenticeship in the scabrous Reeperbahn would have given them every opportunity to explore life's seamier side. The

Beatles grew up in an era when the entertainment press was more discreet and accommodating than it is now. Adversarial tabloid journalism certainly existed, but it was not so prevalent as it is today. And never mind the Internet. Gone are the days when youthful indiscretions could be swept under the rug. Google's CEO has a simple piece of advice for those who wish to escape their online past: change your name!

If you become successful enough, there will be those who want you to fail. They will await any slip up. And now a single indiscretion can blow up years later, worldwide. And there are always people—sometimes extremely attractive people—who will not walk away from a fool and his money.

You do what you've got to do to hit those high notes. But take care not to hurt your family, your reputation, or your business in the process.

92
Children

At some point during the growth and development of the business, you may consider the growth and development of a family. The expansion of the family occurs much like that of the business: a partner at first, then later one or more untrained, inexperienced newbies who will cry about virtually everything when they're not sleeping or eating. It is, however, much different when they are your children.

As they grow and learn, the youngsters will come to understand what it is you do in order to allow them to do what they do. Some may choose to follow your footsteps, while others may not. You may or may not want them to. Remember that it's their call.

In the case of the Beatles, John and his first wife, Cynthia, had a child named Julian for whom Paul wrote the song "Hey Jude." Julian also inspired the song "Lucy in the Sky with Diamonds" when, as a child, he brought home a picture he had drawn and announced to his father that the figure in the work was his schoolmate Lucy, in the sky with diamonds. With Yoko, John had a son they named Sean for whom the song "Beautiful Boy" was written. This song is regarded by many, including McCartney, as one of Lennon's greatest pieces.

Some who are in the arena of growing a business view kids as a drain or distraction. But the fact that some of the Beatles' best songs were the direct or indirect result of having kids speaks volumes. With no offspring, there would be no "Hey Jude," "Lucy in the Sky with Diamonds," or "Beautiful Boy." Likewise, in your pursuits, children may enrich your life, including your professional life, in ways that you may find hard to imagine now. As these children grow and mature, you may well be as gratified by their success as you are by your own. As a recording artist, Julian had two songs to chart in the U.S. and Europe—"Valotte" and "Much Too Late for Goodbyes." Sean likewise has garnered critical acclaim for his songwriting and performing.

Paul and Linda's kids are another success story. Daughter Stella has become one of the most successful and highly regarded fashion designers in the world and has garnered numerous "Designer of the Year" awards from New York to London. Consistent with the vegetarian ethos of the McCartney household, none of her work includes animal skins or furs. Their daughter Heather is a talented pottery designer who was described by Wedgewood as "one of

Britain's new talents" and has received glowing reviews, as has her sister Mary who has followed her mother's path into photography. Son James McCartney is a brilliant guitarist and has written wonderful songs.

The son of Olivia and George Harrison, Dhani Harrison, was introduced to the world at the "Concert For George" where he played guitar and held his own with the likes of Eric Clapton, Jeff Lynne, Tom Petty, Albert Lee, and Joe Brown. A spitting image of his father—the elder Harrison once reportedly told him "You look more like George Harrison than I do"—they collaborated during the final years of George's life in reworking some of George's earlier songs and writing and recording new material.

Maureen and Ringo had a son named Zak who grew into one of the most in-demand drummers in the world, touring with such bands as Oasis and the Who. Zak's brother, Jason, is also a drummer and has worked with a number of successful acts. Lee Starkey, the daughter of Maureen and Ringo, has made her name as a makeup artist.

The moral: as a creative, dynamic parent, you will raise creative, dynamic children. May the apple not fall far from the tree!

93

Take Inventory

If you are like the Beatles, or at least three of them, then with the passage of time, exercises that were so exciting in the early going have become mundane. Outside the group, intriguing opportunities abound that stimulate the creative soul. Recording engineer Richard Dodd stated that "individually, the Beatles were brilliant. Together, they were impossible."

Is that where you are? It could be time to consider a move—a merger, a sale, or to simply cease operations. (A merger is usually a sale, inasmuch as in a short period of time the "target"—a telling term—has been swallowed up by the acquirer and become unrecognizable. To the victor go the spoils.) But first, take a look at where you are, and not just in terms of a profit-and-loss statement or a balance sheet. Can you do the things that bring you enjoyment and income better somewhere else? The answer could be *no*. The greener grass may be a mirage. This can be a disappointing realization.

You may be overlooking positive aspects of the partnership. Is there anything to salvage? Have you begun to take things for granted that may actually be necessary if you are to do your best work? For example, Richard Dodd also noted that "anyone with a modicum of talent could walk in a room and play 'Yesterday' and it would come out fine." Meaning the song was so great no performance could ruin it. But what about "Scrambled Eggs"—the original title? Could the same be said? Without George Martin encouraging Paul to finish the song, would there have been a "Yesterday" at all?

This raises a number of interesting "what if" questions. With the influence of George Martin or even John Lennon, how would "Silly Love Songs" have sounded? What if Paul had been there to take the edge off of John's *Sometime in New York City?* Although George's breakthrough *All Things Must Pass* was a sign of his great, overlooked talent, what if John and Paul had been there to assist? Sadly, for the Beatles, there would be no answers to the "what ifs." Lennon's death meant that there would never be full personal or creative rapprochement among the Beatles.

Happily, if you're reading this book, you are still in the game. Don't underestimate the life that may remain in the old horse. And don't overestimate the time that remains. Fate may soon take the decision out of your hands.

94

Life at the Top

Sometimes it's not so lonely at the top. Ask the Beatles. As Tony Bramwell noticed, people refused to let them buy their own meals, sent them drinks, and gave them virtually anything they wanted when they shopped. If someone did allow a Beatle to write a check for something, the payee never cashed the check. According to Bramwell, the checks were kept for the autograph.

Most of us can't imagine walking down the street only to see hundreds of the best friends we've never met. The principals of any business must be careful, however, especially if they have gone into business with friends. Sometimes, tough decisions must be made that involve people's livelihoods. If there are inadequate boundaries between the personal and the professional, it can get messy.

Many a company has lost its shirt due to executives letting their guard down around other employees and sharing sensitive information that could make its way to the press or the competition if that person leaves, or is mistreated.

The Beatles were in some ways better buddies than bosses. Just as they had relied upon Brian Epstein to fire Pete Best, when it came time to do the dirty work of pruning the Apple tree, they hired Allen Klein. Many of the staff who were made redundant were good Beatle friends, or at least, people who might have expected personal attention to soften the blow. Instead, they received rather peremptory instructions from Klein that amounted to "clean out your desk by five o'clock" (if they, in fact, had a desk). Many were left feeling ill-used by their erstwhile buddies and bosses. There are numerous books written by former employees of the Beatles that reveal, in most cases, their dirty laundry.

There is nothing wrong with relying on third parties to execute staffing decisions or other important business decisions. Where the Beatles erred was by cultivating an overfamiliar workplace, one in which firing somebody seemed on some level an unimaginable violation of trust and friendship rather than a sound, if unfortunate, financial decision.

There is a difference between being a convivial employer and being a personal friend. Make sure you understand that difference and do not cross the line between them.

95
Perspective

When the enterprise was in its start-up phase, everything was magnified: every negotiation, every unexpected objection, every appointment was filled with surprises, the closing of every deal seemingly fraught with difficulty and conflict.

As time passes and the deals accumulate, you come to expect the unexpected, and handle it. No two gigs are alike, no two deals alike. Although all contain similarities, there will be specifics that pertain only to that particular situation. But with long experience in the arena, these issues are not as bothersome. On the positive side, there is less drama and stress; however, there is also less excitement. You have discovered that there really is nothing to get hung about. Some transactions will fail. All businesses make mistakes. It's part of the process. Partners should not carry grudges against each other over long-gone mistakes.

Brian Epstein is often vilified for his early contract and merchandising negotiations in his representation of the Beatles. In an earlier chapter, we discussed the long-term effect of the millions that were lost, and the importance of competent negotiation and adequate professional representation. Yet, as Shakespeare, another talented Englishman, once wrote, "The evil that men do lives after them; the good is oft interred with their bones." Even with Epstein's alleged shortcomings, the four Liverpool musicians who were barely scraping out a living while living with their parents or relatives were able to become multimillionaires in their twenties. We must remember to praise Epstein's incredible achievement.

As many who have made it and lost it or made it and retained it say, "It's only money." There are always opportunities to earn more, especially after a disaster or two. If a deal goes south, learn from that transaction, get back on the horse, and try something else. Failure paralyzes some, but it inspires you and others like you. Behind every success is a failure. Ahead of every success is another stumble. It's simply a part of life, unless you choose to be, in the words of Teddy Roosevelt, one of the "cold and timid souls who know neither victory nor defeat."

96

The Unconditionally Loyal

As any enterprise expands from the original person or part-ners, the first hire is generally one of the best employees the group will ever have. The person is usually well known by the founder, or even by several of the founders.

This person was there when there was very little capital, poor working conditions, and every day was a struggle. Many of these early employees possess an entrepreneurial gene or two of their own; they may even start to flex their entrepreneur-ial muscles while still in your employ. These folks will do fine no matter what happens to your company. Others, who may be focused simply on doing whatever it takes to keep the com-pany and its principals happy, may have trouble adjusting to life beyond the rarefied atmosphere they have come to enjoy as a trusted lieutenant.

In the case of the Beatles there were several early key employees. First was Neil Aspinall, who was a close friend of Pete Best, but, on Pete's recommendation and with his blessing, stayed on after Pete was released. Neil's duties in the early days included driving his van with the Beatles as passengers to the gigs, unloading the gear, and setting the stage. By the time of his death, he had become the president of Apple and ran the company flawlessly. The *Anthology* was his brainchild. He produced that wildly successful and extraordinarily profitable multi-media success, which gave rise to a number-one best-selling book, several albums that topped the charts, a top-rated television series, and a best-selling DVD collection, amassing hundreds of millions of dollars in all.

Tony Bramwell was also involved early on, carrying the guitars of George and Paul to the gigs in order to be admitted at no charge. He accompanied the Beatles on many a cold, dark night in the van with Neil and later Mal Evans. An offhand genius, Bramwell created the music video in the 1960s as a way for the Beatles to be on TV without traveling. He had the Beatles perform their new songs for three cameras and, at a cost of no more than 750 pounds, produced videos of the songs which he sold to television shows such as *Hollywood Palace, Shindig, Hullaballoo, American Bandstand,* and similar production companies across the world for as much as $10,000 each. (The Beatles would also loan Bramwell out to other artists to provide the same benefit for a tidy sum.) Tony sharpened his marketing skills and made significant contacts in the music world while working at Apple and has been able to parlay those skills into a successful career. He continues to work with Paul McCartney on various projects.

Another key employee, Mal Evans, found life after the Beatles to be more difficult. Evans, the lovable, giant of a bouncer, bodyguard, stagehand, driver, and professional friend, was with them from the Cavern days and appears in *Let It Be* as well as *Help!* Constantly on hand, he played the anvil in "Maxwell's Silver Hammer," counted off "A Day in the Life," and claimed to have participated in the writing of "Fixing a Hole." Sadly, he was shot and killed by Los Angeles policemen who approached him after he was described by a female friend as being drugged and depressed. He was wielding an unloaded air gun at the time.

In the closing of an office, partnership, or company, time should be taken to assess the psychological condition of those left behind or outside. People like Mal Evans participated in a journey that included only the Beatles and a handful of others. Some, such as Bramwell, leave relieved and ready to take on the world, while others leave saddened, hurt, and unprepared. Officially, they are owed nothing, but a friendly pep talk, perhaps some training, or a recommendation to other employment can go a long way.

97
Passing the Torch

With the Beatles, this torch was passed relatively early, while they were still in their twenties (Lennon and Starr both turned thirty in 1970), after just ten years of partnership.

As with any group of such enormous influence, the "heirs" to the Beatles were many and stretched beyond music. Harrison himself was rumored to have said that the spirit of the Beatles had passed into the Monty Python comedy troupe, whose absurd ensemble comedy became a phenomenon on both sides of the Atlantic in the 1970s.

In some ways, however, the Beatles were their own successors, continuing to write and perform in a way that could not help being ever so slightly Beatle-esque. Each was handed the same legacy, but they all embarked on different journeys—John to try changing the world through his actions and his music, Paul perhaps to be bigger than the Beatles and make the world better in a less contentious manner, George to show the world he was better than Beatle George and to find inner peace, and Ringo to continue being Ringo, making hit records and performing on the road.

At some point, it will be appropriate to step down or aside and allow others to carry on. This could happen in a matter of months or after years. If the torch you pass allows your former group to change the world, with your employees and protégés producing great works, and others inspired by your example to take up their own journeys, you will have truly succeeded Beatle-style.

98
Rest

The assassination of John Lennon had a significant effect on the three surviving Beatles. All had worried about security, especially in the 1960s, but they had begun to feel more at ease with world. After Lennon was gunned down, each of the others realized that another of them could have been the target. It would make sense to stop and smell the roses (in Harrison's case, quite literally, having cultivated a knack for gardening in his later years).

We probably don't have to look too far around us for similar examples. Although we may not deal with a murder, in non-Beatle life there are colleagues, friends, and acquaintances dying of cancer, heart disease, and an assortment of other ailments often caused by stress, lack of rest, and poor eating habits often associated with overwork.

When you are weary, you are not as sharp as when you are free of fatigue, be it mental, psychological, or physical. There are those who work better under pressure, or deadlines, but only if they are well rested over the long term. By resting, you can begin to rebuild your body, mind, and psyche. Remember the workout analogy: the muscle is repaired and capacity is built up during the rest period after the actual exercise itself, which in fact imposes wear and tear on the tissue. In a similar way, these fallow professional periods can in fact be quite productive.

In the case of the Beatles, it was during their long down time that they compiled the *Anthology*. It required an extraordinary amount of research and work, but only two new songs (achieving, finally, a reunion of sorts), a few interviews, and a "jam" session. It became their most profitable single project—twenty-five years after their formal dissolution.

99

Retirement

Retirement need only be from a job, not from life itself. Even if your job was being a Beatle, there are alternative, meaningful outlets that can enable you to have a more positive impact on yourself, your family, your community, and the world after retiring from the rat race.

Like millions of Beatle fans worldwide, Paul McCartney always seemed to cherish a small hope that there would be a reunion, or at least an understanding, between him and Lennon. It almost came to pass, according to May Pang, who spent eighteen months with John on his "lost weekend" when Yoko banished him from the Dakota. Pang was with Lennon when he signed the Beatles' dissolution agreement. She said that once the contract was executed, John felt such a relief that he was not contractually bound to Paul, that they began to rebuild their relationship and even made plans to work together again. (This is an object lesson in itself of the importance of letting go.) Shortly after that emotion overtook Lennon, Yoko allowed him to return home, and the reunion never occurred.

Retirement seemed to suit John especially; he spent the first five years of his son Sean's life in the self-described capacity of "house husband." The role served him well and allowed him to understand the hardships endured in parenting to little or no acclaim. As he noted, there were no awards for baking a great loaf of bread.

In the last several years of his life, George Harrison had taken to gardening and developed a passion for growing things. Ringo toured constantly, working with different musicians in his All Starr Band or the Roundheads.

And Sir Paul? He may never retire. His zest for writing and performing music seems unabated, and his awareness of encroaching age seems to have provided additional incentive to keep going while he still can. Long may he rock!

100
The End

One should always begin with the End in mind. The Beatles were the biggest, most influential group of musicians in history. The amount of joy and happiness that they brought, and continue to bring to untold millions is incalculable. No one can diminish or second-guess their unparalleled creative output. Geniuses in the right place at the right time, young Midases competing in a famously unstructured business, influenced by the freewheeling ethos of the 60s, with its myriad "happenings," they could never imagine that one could—and should—adopt a more proactive attitude in the management of one's affairs. They indeed let life "happen" to them, with sometimes disastrous results.

If they had one major flaw, that was it: an unwillingness, or inability, to plan effectively for life's inevitable contingencies, including death. They can hardly be blamed. Keep in mind that the oldest Beatles, Ringo and John, were just thirty years old when the Beatles officially disbanded. Thirty!

They never had a chance. But you do. Your business does. Make sure that all the partners in your business know how it will end. There should be clear agreements about buying or selling interests in the business, to each other or to third parties. These agreements should be secured with comprehensive insurance policies, so that if one partner dies, the heirs will not suddenly need to come up with the cash to buy out the other partners, or (worse) come seeking cash from the business, or (worst of all) be motivated to sell their interest in the business to (potentially adverse) third parties. (In other words, make sure the personal affairs and finances of the deceased partner have minimal impact on the continued operations of the business. Think Brian Epstein!)

There should also be clear succession planning, so that if a partner dies or leaves, there is a clear way forward for the business and for the other partners. What happens when George or John quits the band? What happens when you die? Don't let it paralyze the business. Once they have mourned, the best way they can honor you is for your successors to keep moving the business forward. Make sure every partner has adequate life and disability insurance and a clear, idiot-proof last will and testament.

Once you have taken these precautions, enjoy the ride. The End will come soon enough, as it already has for so many who shared the Beatles' wild ride: Stuart Sutcliffe, Brian Epstein, John

Lennon, Alistair Taylor, George Harrison, Linda McCartney, Allen Klein, Maureen Starkey, Mal Evans, Neil Aspinall, Billy Preston, Peter Brown, Dick James, Norman "Hurricane" Smith, and others.

It has been said that you write your own obituary. You do so through your actions, words, and in the works you leave behind. May your epitaph read, "Bigger than the Beatles!"

Index

Index

Index

Index

making *Sgt. Peppers* album, 153-55; solo work for Apple Records, 221; tours with other bands, 288. *See also* Beatles; Roundheads, the; Storm, Rory, and the Hurricanes

Storm, Rory, and the Hurricanes, 16, 37, 40, 41

"Strawberry Fields Forever" (Lennon for Beatles), 113, 132

Sutcliffe, Stuart (Stu), 290; member of Quarrymen, 11; "Mop Top" haircut, 21; leaves the band, 23-24, 206

Swaggart, Jimmy, 166

Swettenham, Dick (Olympic recording engineer), 190, 191

Swirsky, Seth (Beatles documentarian), 158

Talley, Gary (Box Tops), 83-84

Tandy, 54

"Taxman" (Harrison for Beatles), 74, 99

Taylor, Alistair, 291

Taylor, James, 221

Thomas, Dave, and Wendy's, 13

Tillich, Paul, 236

Tin Pan Alley, 82

Toft, Malcolm (Trident recording engineer), 190, 191

Tolle, Eckhart, 173

"Toppermost of the Poppermost." *See* Beatles

Toyota, 55

Traveling Wilburys, 94

Troy, Doris, 254

"Twenty Flight Rock" (Eddie Cochran), 10

Two Virgins (Lennon and Ono album), 208

"Uncle Albert/Admiral Halsey" (McCartney solo single), 236

Undertakers, the, 16, 28

United Artists: signs Beatles to film, 59

"Valotte" (Julian Lennon single), 272

Volkswagen Beetle, 20

Voormann, Klaus, 21, 40, 141, 206, 255

Wal-Mart, 13

Walton, Sam, and Wal-Mart, 13

Wedding Album, The (Lennon and Ono album), 255

Wendy's, 13

"While My Guitar Gently Weeps" (Harrison for Beatles), 232

White, Alan, 255

White Album, The (Beatles album), 172, 200, 202, 229, 232, 248

Who, the, 94, 141, 273

Williams, Alan (Beatles manager), 77

Wilson, Brian, and the Beach Boys, 97

Wilson, Harold, 222

"With a Little Help from My Friends" (Beatles), 41

Woolton Fete, 11, 78

Wozniak, Steve, and Apple Computers, 12

Yardbirds, 242

"Yellow Submarine" (Beatles), 41; meaning of, 168

Yellow Submarine (Beatles album), 229

"Yesterday" (McCartney for Beatles), 61-62, 68, 243, 275; and string quartet accompaniment, 93, 128-29

"You Can't Do That" (Beatles), 88

"You Know My Name (Look Up The Number)" (Beatles), 168

"You've Got to Hide Your Love Away" (Beatles), 94, 134

Zapple (Beatles company), 220

Zombies, the, 141